THE CUBAN WAY

To my parents Braulio and Belkys,
also in memory of my grandfather, Cruz Alonso,
who taught me the values of freedom and solidarity.

PREFACE

Nothing can be loved or hated until it is first known.
Leonardo Da Vinci, 1500[1]

It would be just a matter of days. The Soviet Union had fallen, and socialist Cuba was sure to follow. At least that's what the United States predicted. The rest of the world thought so too. Even Cubans were wondering what would come next.

To the surprise of all, the disappointment of many, and the joy of a few, Cuba and its socialist government defied the odds: they survived. What happened? How did they confront an economic debacle that sliced almost forty percent off the economy in four years? How did they sidestep the precipice? How long can the balancing act last?

Much has been written about the Cuban experience these days as scores of analysts try to answer these questions. However, the literature on Cuba tends to be either highly technical and scholarly[2] or tainted with biases that distort the picture. This is particularly true in Washington, where I have lived for the past four years. The tendency is to oversimplify the debates about Latin America in general, and Cuba in particular. A highly polarized ideological environment has limited the possibilities for unbiased analysis by substituting the need to understand with the desire to score political points. The categories are simple dichotomies: pro or against the embargo; pro or against Fidel; left or right; right or wrong.

The purpose of this book is to share with you my analysis of the situation, based on personal experience rather than political ideology. I have been to the island many times, talking to intellectuals, government officials, and people on the street, listening to their ideas, frustrations, and hopes. My objective is not to judge Cubans, but to understand them. Is Cuba a monolithic society where everyone thinks alike? How repressed do they feel? How do they view their problems? What trade-offs do they perceive? What do Cubans disagree on? What do they think about their government? How do they view the United States? What do they do for fun? I wanted to understand how this country on the brink of collapse managed to avoid its destiny.

While I am not in the ideological game, I confess to a personal history that has necessarily shaped my point of view. This book responds to a professional and personal passion, if not a political one. Writing about Cuba became an urge soon after I returned from my first trip to the island in 1995. I am a Venezuelan, born in Cuba, who left the island at two years of age and went back to rediscover it. I am a Latin American born in the fifties. My family suffered the typical wanderings of those difficult political times. My mother, and all of her family, are Cuban. My father is Venezuelan. He met my mother in Havana in 1949 while he was a political exile from a Venezuelan dictator. In 1953, we left Cuba because another dictator, Batista, was making my father's life intolerable. After a few bouts in jail and continuous harassment by security agents, he had to leave, once again, for another country. My mother was a Cuban middle-class law student who shared the University of Havana classrooms with Fidel Castro. She had never thought about exile and its profound psychological implications until she met my father.

When the three of us left Havana in 1953, my mother never imagined the nightmare that was to come. Seven years later, her parents and the rest of her family—stripped of everything they owned—would also be leaving Cuba to escape the successful socialist revolution headed by her onetime classmate, Fidel Castro. Among the things my grandfather had to leave behind was his hotel, the San Luis. Situated half a block from Havana's boardwalk, the *Malecon*, the San Luis had been his business for almost two decades. I returned to the same place in 1995 to find two hundred families living within its deteriorated walls.

"Since all the rooms were designed with a small kitchen and bath, they decided to turn it into an apartment building," said the administrator. He knew my grandfather and remembered him with respect and affection. He apologized for living in the same apartment my grandparents had lived in for almost two decades. "I know how you must feel," I heard him saying while I was struggling to understand my own feelings.

The San Luis Hotel was well known to Venezuelan exiles. In one of its rooms, the famous Venezuelan novelist and ex-president, Romulo Gallegos, lived and wrote his novel, *Una Brizna de Paja en el Viento*. Venezuelan poet Andrés Eloy Blanco conceived some of the poems from his book *Poda* there, and ex-presidents Romulo Betancourt and Carlos Andrés Pérez met there frequently to dream and plan their return to dictator-free Venezuela.

That was the environment I grew up in. The difference between democracies and dictatorships was not something you learned at school; it was part of your everyday life, the stories told and retold at the dinner table each night.

The political dreams of the times were clear: freedom, democracy, and social justice. Little did we know of the difficult trade-offs inherent in such an attractive but complex mix. Today, all countries in the region—except Cuba—enjoy multiparty democracies. But Latin America is still the continent with the greatest inequality in the World.

For all these reasons it has been a fascinating experience to write about the economic and political realities facing Cubans during the past four decades. I know that that many will wonder about the reliability of the numbers and statistics I used to analyze the Cuban economy. There is in fact very little international scrutiny of Cuban economic figures and methodologies since Cuba is not a member of institutions such as the World Bank or the International Monetary Fund. Despite that fact, there is much we can learn about the Cuban experience since there is also very little knowledge about the way Cubans have managed economic and social changes in the same period.

   This book is an effort to fill a huge vacuum. While statistics on Cuba may be hard to find, the trends, the consequences, the reality and the personal stories are *there*. A good analysis is more than numbers. And that's what I've tried to do with this book: add faces to the numbers, and images to the charts. I've tried to tell an economic story based on my analysis and the words of Cubans living that story today.[3]

Notes

1. Leonardo Da Vinci, *Note Books*, (1500) Jean Paul Ritcher. In *The International Thesaurus of Quotations*. (New York: HarperCollins Publishers, Inc., 1996).
2. For in-depth economic analyses see bibliography.
3. All stories told in this book are based on true accounts.

THE SAME, BUT DIFFERENT

> Cuba must open to the World and the World must
> open to Cuba.
>
> Pope John Paul II
> Havana, January 21, 1998[1]

Pope John Paul II spoke these words during his historic visit to Cuba—
an event that indicates Cuba is already undergoing the opening process
he referred to. But while Cuba is beginning to peek out from behind its
personal iron curtain, it remains essentially alone and isolated, the last
bulwark of communism in the Western World and one of the last on the
planet. In one word, Cuba is different—from its neighbors, and from
the rest of the world.

But Cuba wasn't always the exception to the hemispheric rule. In
fact, in the 1950s it was very much one of the crowd. When the Cuban
revolution overthrew the Batista regime, Cuba was just one more example of Latin American radicalism. The political platform of the Cuban
revolutionary movement mirrored the ideological mood throughout the
region. From Mexico to Argentina, the slogans were the same. The prevalent ideology was labeled "leftist" or "socialist." In retrospect, however,
it seems less radical. The agenda was basically political freedom, nationalism, and a strong government capable of promoting economic
growth and greater equality in the most inequitable region in the world.
Why did Cuba radicalize?

Leaving Cuba

Don Cruz was leaving Cuba, and this time he was leaving for good.
He loved the Island, but he didn't like what was happening around him.
It was 1960 and the revolution he had supported was getting out of
hand; he could see the political radicalization of the regime unfolding.

While imagining his life away from Cuba, a voice brought him back

1

to reality. "Don Cruz, the taxi is outside waiting. You have to leave now or you'll miss your plane." His friend, the hotel's administrator, unaware of the real reason for his trip, was urging him to leave.

That morning, the bright Havana sun was even brighter and the air coming from the sea had the familiar smell Cruz had learned to love. It had been fifteen years since he bought the San Luis hotel a block away from the *Malecon*. While glancing at the familiar view from his room in the hotel, he remembered what Jorge the *miliciano*[2] had said: "If you don't like the way we're managing things around here Cruz, you're free to leave."

And that's what he was doing. Yes, it was difficult for him to imagine life without that view, that smell, that feeling of belonging and familiarity. "We know you helped the revolution, so you must understand," Jorge had said. "Under the real estate reform, some of the rooms will be used for the homeless. We might even have to turn this hotel into an apartment building. We need homes, not tourists."

Cruz knew what was going on. According to the new policy, housing was a priority. Those who left had their assets confiscated by the state, and those who stayed were occupying the confiscated assets. As the dicey political situation scared tourists away, hotel rooms were increasingly empty while the government needed more housing. "Everybody must have a place to live; you'll keep your home, nobody will touch it," assured Jorge, trying to please him.

The *miliciano* didn't know that for Cruz, the hotel was his home. In fact, it was his life. He had lived in one of those rooms for fifteen years. Some of his grandchildren were born there. "No problem, you can keep the rooms you've been using. Come on, Cruz, you'll get the hotel back," Jorge had explained after realizing his mistake. But Cruz knew he'd never get it back. In fact, he knew he was in command of neither his business nor his home anymore. Yes, he had to leave, things were going in a different direction than he had expected when he backed Fidel.

In less than two years, the Cuban revolution was turning into a communist revolution. Confrontation with former friends, including Fidel, was inevitable. He wasn't going to stick around for it. He couldn't help the flashbacks of his own life.

Don Cruz had left poverty behind in the Canary Islands almost half a century ago. At fifteen years of age he arrived in Cuba looking for a land of opportunities, and he had found it. Without a university degree, he saw his four children graduate at the University of Havana. He had worked his way up from delivering groceries in a small town, to owning and managing a nice hotel in Havana. From his room at the hotel, he

A taxicycle draped in the American flag drives by the former San
Luis Hotel, now home to 200 families.

could admire the Caribbean Sea. He loved Cuba, a country he had made
his own. He had suffered with Cuba's political problems. He was a
democrat; he believed in freedom and he had put his money where his
mouth was. He had hosted in his hotel social democrats in exile from
throughout Latin America. He had received and shared dreams of

freedom with them. From Venezuela, Guatemala, the Dominican Republic, many escaping right-wing dictators in their homeland, exiles found a home at the San Luis in Havana. He also knew Fidel; he had spoken with him. He had heard them all. They all sounded the same, their political agendas, their personal stories. The objectives were similar: to overthrow the dictators, achieve political freedom, promote social justice, and boost economic growth for the benefit of all.

Now he was going to Venezuela. He had family and friends there. His son-in-law, a Venezuelan exile who married his oldest daughter in Havana, was now a senator in his country. His friends, former exiles and guests in his hotel, were now members of parliament and of a so-cial democratic government. With a political agenda similar to Fidel's, a revolutionary movement in Venezuela had overthrown a right-wing dictator just a year before Fidel's rebel forces overthrew Batista. The parallels of the past were evident; but the future looked starkly differ-ent. While Venezuela was democratizing, Cuba was radicalizing. What had happened? Cruz had his own theory that Cuba was turning social-ist; there was no middle way and because of it, he was leaving.

Socialist Cuba in Socialist Latin America

Following the Great Depression, the importance of creating social safety nets for workers and the poor became a worldwide concern. Latin America was no exception to this trend. The economies of the region had been predominantly export oriented and liberal, with open trade and low tariffs. Most countries specialized in the production and ex-port of commodities: corn, sugar, coffee, meat, oil, copper and bananas, among others. Everything else was imported. Land was highly concen-trated in the hands of foreign investors and local elites. With the Great Depression, international prices for commodities collapsed and with it the region's most important source of hard currency. Everyone in Latin America took a share of the loss, but those with little to lose were left with nothing. The desperation of many turned into social discontent, and the time was ripe for political change.

One of the first targets of discontent was the alliance between for-eign investors and local elites in producing and exporting commodities. For most, it was a deal that smacked of exploitation and injustice. True or false, the majority thought the terms of trade were unfair and that foreign investors were depleting the country's resources while neglect-ing workers' welfare. Nationalism was a natural outgrowth of opposition to an economic strategy based on foreign investment and commodity exports. Since U.S. investment was dominant in the region, so too were strong anti-U.S. feelings. Within this context, certain "revolutionary" ideas began to gain a foothold: agrarian reform to redistribute land, nationalization of industries, and the creation of safety nets for workers. Given the economic and social climate, all of these goals appeared reasonable and understandable.

A new leadership without ties to the traditional elites or foreign investors increasingly spoke out in favor of economic change and social justice. A new ideology, which defended the incorporation of the masses into the economic, social, and political life of their countries, soon found many followers. Their words and ideas resounded throughout the region—and Cuba was no exception.

The ideology of the 1950s, in Cuba and throughout Latin America, is difficult to define in terms of classic cold-war and post–cold-war polarities. That is why many analysts argue that the first stage of the Cuban revolution "lacked a clearly defined ideology."[3] New demands for social justice were turning the tide of history in Latin America, as country after country struggled to incorporate new societal groups into the political landscape. Many of the ideals advocated by the new Cuban regime had already been debated in capitals throughout the region. Contrary to its image today, Cuba was not marching to a different drummer. It was right in step in the regional parade."

In Step with Anti-communist Peron

Juan Domingo Perón (1946–1955) initiated a broad restructuring of the Argentine economy that greatly resembled the early reforms of the Castro regime in Cuba. Perón, however, was an adamant anti-communist and was even considered by many to be semi-fascist. A brief review of his economic policies shows they echo those of Cuba and demonstrates that labels like *fascist* and *communist* lose meaning in the context of a region-wide shift toward nationalism, state-centralized economic power, and income redistribution. Perón also proceeded with nationalizations: the railroad system, gas, telephone, airlines, the merchant fleet, and electrical companies.[4] Clearly, the discourse in Argentina and Cuba was very much the same. Perhaps the greatest difference was the foreign investor that received the brunt of their nationalist fury: in Argentina, it was Great Britain; in Cuba, it was the United States.

In Step with Nationalists in Peru

Victor Raul Haya de la Torre and his American Popular Revolutionary Alliance (APRA) championed a similar economic and social agenda: anti-imperialism, economic and political regionalism, agrarian reform, nationalization of industries such as oil, internationalization of the Panama Canal,[5] establishment of an eight-hour workday, and programs of universal and bilingual education to incorporate the indigenous population into society. In many ways, APRA's political platform typified the political sentiment that swept across the region after the Great Depression.

In Step with Social Democrats in Venezuela

The ideological background and substance of the dominant Democratic Action (AD) program was quite similar to APRA's. In 1947–48, AD's first president, Romulo Gallegos, enacted important reforms in health, education, wages, and industrial development, including a 50/50 tax reform formula for revenue sharing for foreign investors in the oil industry. The aggressive set of reforms was too much for the status quo and a military coup ended the short-lived AD administration in October 1948. Venezuela had to wait another ten years for its next democratic elections. When AD won again in 1959, an agrarian reform that included land expropriation was enacted. Where Venezuela's AD party differed from Cuba's revolutionary movement was in its advocacy of change through democracy, but the ideological camaraderie was evident at both the policy and the popular levels:

> At the end of January 1959, he (Fidel) flew to Caracas in his first foreign trip as the victorious revolutionary leader to thank Admiral Larrazabal and the ruling Venezuelan government junta for dispatching arms to the Sierra Maestra in 1958. He also called on president-elect Romulo Betancourt despite the contempt he had for him as reformist (and not revolutionary) of the Latin American "Democratic Left." Venezuelans, liberated from dictatorship a year earlier, gave Castro a deliriously happy reception.[6]

In Step with Leftist Guatemala

The Guatemalan experience was an important lesson for Cuban revolutionaries. Argentine-turned-Cuban revolutionary, Ernesto "Che" Guevara, was living in Guatemala in 1952, when President Jacobo Arbenz initiated a similar program there. It began with an agrarian reform with land expropriation in a country where 2.2 percent of the population owned seventy percent of the land[7] and included labor reforms such as minimum wage laws, the creation of the Social Security Institute to develop a safety net, and universal free education.

As later happened in Cuba, the Arbenz government touched important U.S. interests. In 1954, Jacobo Arbenz was toppled thanks to "Operation Success," a U.S. invasion led by Guatemalan dissident Castillo Armas and manned by Guatemalan exiles. United Fruit Company played an important role in this government takeover and demonstrated the power of American business. After rejecting the compensation offered by the Guatemalan government, United Fruit launched a public relations campaign hiring "a corps of influential lobbyists and talented publicists to create a public and private climate in the United States favorable to Arbenz's overthrow."[8] Castillo Armas assumed power from June 1954 until his assassination in July 1957. The lessons of the frustrated Arbenz government were not lost on "el Che."

In Step with Revolutionary Bolivia

Bolivia too, had much in common with Cuba. The Movimiento Nacional Revolucionario (MNR) that assumed power in a virtually bloodless revolution in 1952 resembled the 1959 Cuban regime in that they were both victorious rebel forces with strongly nationalistic programs. Both rejected foreign domination of their economies and called for abolishing "imperialism." Agrarian reform was a key element in both regimes' economic programs; both viewed it as a means of redistributing wealth and improving agricultural productivity. The most important sectors of the economy were nationalized, including the mines, and the old elite-dominated systems were dismantled. Both governments created a centralized economy, championed workers' rights, and attacked corruption. Despite the similarities, the U.S. reaction to the revolutions varied dramatically. Washington terminated relations with Cuba while it strengthened its ties to the Bolivian government in the months following the revolution.

Part of the explanation for the apparently schizophrenic attitude of the United States lies in the magnitude of its economic exposure in each country. While the United States feared the nationalization of U.S. property in both countries, the extent of its investments was far greater in Cuba than in Bolivia.[9] In Bolivia, the three major tin mines, which were the backbone of the economy, were owned by Bolivians. Only one of these corporations had U.S. stockholders. For example, the per capita book value of U.S. enterprises in Cuba in 1959 was more than three times that of the rest of Latin America: US$143 for every Cuban versus US$39 per inhabitant in the rest of the region.[10] When the government went ahead and nationalized the mines, the United States sat idly by, instead of using force as it later did in Guatemala and Cuba. There was no intervention and two years later elections were called.

The experience of the Bolivian revolution provides important clues to the apparent mystery of Cuban radicalization. If the ideological climate was the same, what made Cuba's affair with socialism so different from the rest of Latin America's? What were the circumstances, internal and external, that turned Fidel and his followers into radical communists? When faced with the trade-offs, why did the outgoing, freedom-loving, salsa-dancing Cubans choose the boredom and monotony of communism?

To a large extent, the answer to these questions lies in Cuba's peculiar relationship—past and present—with the United States. And the key to Cuba's future, including the prospects for its nascent reform program, lie in resolving the outstanding issues derived from this relationship. In this light, a more accurate adaptation of Pope John Paul II's historic words could be: Cuba must open to the United States and the United States must open to Cuba.

Basically, there are two factors that distinguish Cuba from the rest of Latin America. The first is a sort of hyper-nationalism provoked largely by the involvement of the United States in Cuba's relatively late independence movement from Spain. The second, which is closely intertwined with the first, derives from the profound economic ties between the two countries—a situation that made the geopolitical implications of Cuba's flirtations with the left quite different from those of the rest of Latin America. The issue, which is still very much outstanding, is the property rights of both Cubans and U.S. citizens over Cuban assets.

Frustrated Nationalism

"Why are these Cubans so stubbornly nationalistic" is a common complaint from those who have tried exhaustively to promote a dialogue between the United States and Cuba. Former Attorney General and U.S. Secretary of Defense Elliot Richardson said on his 1995 trip to Cuba that "an excess of pride" on both sides was the main reason for the deadlock in U.S.-Cuba negotiations.

The roots of this nationalistic pride are found in Cuba's tempestuous history. Cuba's achievement of independence from Spain was a lengthy and frustrating process. After ten years of war during the 1870s that proved fruitless for Cuba, the conflict between the two countries was rekindled in 1895. In January 1898, after almost four years of war and with a Cuban victory in sight, U.S. President William McKinley dispatched the battleship *Maine* to Havana for an "extended visit." The United States had seen in the Spanish-Cuban conflict a "possibility of danger to American life and property" and sent its battleship "just in case."[11] The *Maine* exploded a few days later and with it, a war between Spain and the United States over control of Cuba.

The United States defeated Spain handily in just a few months and Cuba became a U.S. protectorate rather than the independent state it had envisioned less than a year earlier. While in 1898 the United States insisted it had no intention of annexing the island, President McKinley refused to recognize the Cuban rebels and their new government. Instead, the Americans set up a military government in Cuba, conditioning the withdrawal of soldiers on Cuban acceptance of the U.S. right to intervene in Cuba "for the maintenance of a government adequate for the protection of life, property, and individual liberties."

The Platt Amendment, which gave the United States this license to intervene, was hated by Cuban nationalists. The treaty granted the United States the right not only to intervene militarily in Cuba but to control Cuba's debts and treaties with other countries and to establish naval bases on the island.[12] Cubans felt deceived by the United States; instead of helping them eradicate colonialism, their northern neighbor had simply imposed a new type of foreign domination. From that moment on, Cuba's twentieth-century history was a series of revolutionary attempts and dictators. Throughout the 1930s there were continuous revolts until nationalists and socialists formed an alliance to support president Ramón Grau Martin, who attempted to grant land to peasants and limit foreign ownership. He was overthrown by a U.S.-backed coup d'état led by Fulgencio Batista in 1934. Immediately afterwards, the United States agreed to abrogate the Platt amendment in order to squelch a groundswell of Cuban nationalism. In 1952, Batista returned to power thanks to yet another U.S.-backed coup d'état.

Although the Spanish-American conflict lasted only a few months at the close of the nineteenth century, the U.S.-Cuban power struggle has endured almost a century and has not yet ended. The U.S. embargo and the recently passed Helms-Burton Law (1996) are seen by Cubans on the island as another manifestation of U.S. intervention in Cuban internal affairs.

Given this history, it is no surprise that Fidel's strong anti-U.S. intervention message struck a sensitive nationalist chord deep within Cubans. His political message was highly nationalist and categorically rejected the political and economic dominance of the United States. Although the sentiment was shared by other countries in Latin America, in Cuba, the feeling was more explosive.

Living in the 50s

It was March 10, 1952. Fulgencio Batista had just taken power by force and Mrs. Preston was on the phone inviting Paula and her husband to a party. But Paula was in the mood for crying, not for partying. Another dictator meant more brutality, more injustice, less hope for them and for the people in the cane fields. What did she have to celebrate about anyway? Her daughter Virginia had answered the phone and had almost forced her to take a call she did not want to answer. "Mom! She insists on talking to you. You know how these Americans are. They think they own the place," insisted Virginia, who at twelve was already a passionate nationalist.

"Paula? Listen, we are having a big party tonight. Why don't you come and celebrate. Batista will be great for us and for the Company. You know, United Fruit has great connections with this government."

Paula couldn't believe her ears. Her husband, Walter, had been working for the United Fruit Company for fifteen years. But she and her husband were Cubans and they were democrats; they did not want a dictator. Walter had an acceptable job as an overseer in one of the Company's sugar cane plantations. Yet their daughter, Virginia, was not accepted in the Company's school. The schools were only for the children of American employees. Since there were no public schools in the area, at the age of eight their child had to leave home and stay with different American families in order to get an elementary education. She had no choice, but she had the hope that some day things would change. At the front door, a skinny *guajiro* from the plantation was trying to sell her an even skinnier chicken "to buy some cooking oil, please." No, she was not in the mood for celebration.

"I'm sorry, but I hope you understand. How would you feel if this had happened in the United States?" Paula dared to ask.

"That's difficult for me to imagine because, you know Paula, something like this could never happen in the United States," answered Mrs. Preston.

Forty-five years later, Virginia remembers as if it were yesterday and with the same rage her mother felt back then, that conversation with Mrs. Preston. She remembers the invitation to celebrate a dictator. She remembers that to go to school in her own country she had to live with Americans. The great educational system Cubans used to rave about was limited to the big cities. In the rural area where she lived, there were no Cuban schools and the Company's school was open to American families only. For Virginia, there were no choices; either she lived with Americans, or didn't go to school.

She also remembers the misery of the *guajiros*. They lived like animals in wooden huts called *barracones* built by The Company, with ten to twelve rooms: one family per room. No bathrooms, no kitchen, they cooked outside with coal. "I can still remember how they used to smell." Sadly enough, the families that lived there, were the "lucky" ones. Those who didn't have *barracones,* had to live outside in the open and if they tried to build a small shack, The Company would call the Rural Guard to come and burn the shacks down.

Virginia still doesn't understand how those people survived the "dead season" between harvests. They were paid for a maximum of three months a year: the period when the sugarcane needed to be cut. The rest of the time they had to survive by planting vegetables for self-consumption, *only* if The Company granted them permission to do so, on minimal plots of land on the fringes of the cane field. There were no schools for their children. The Company provided some health care treatment that later was deducted from their paychecks.

Virginia had hopeful dreams when she heard the revolutionary messages on Radio Rebelde.[13] Her father used to explain to her how things would change with the agrarian reform and how the land would be shared by all. He had been doing the financial calculations for years and had figured out how a cooperative system in those lands would dramatically increase the standard of living for all the *guajiros*. Virginia married a revolutionary, she became a revolutionary herself. After a few years, she left revolutionary Cuba with great disappointment. "But, in spite of all the mistakes, all the frustration, the sufferings and the setbacks, I am convinced today, that the revolution was necessary—it just had to happen."

Who Owns This Country Anyway?

For better or for worse, big fortunes were made under U.S. protection during the first five decades of the century in Cuba. Because of the Platt Amendment, Cuba's sovereign risk was very low, and U.S. investors considered it the safest investment bet in Latin America.

By the 1930s, U.S. firms controlled seventy-five percent of the sugarcane crop in Cuba. Their powerful lobbying in the U.S. Congress not only guaranteed access to the U.S. market but also higher-than-world prices. In addition, with the help of Great Britain, the United States formed a sugar consumer cartel. Cuba was basically a one-crop economy tied to only one buyer.

The burgeoning U.S. investment in Cuba generated an alliance between U.S. investors, the U.S. government and the Cuban economic elite. By the time of the revolution, the United States controlled forty percent of sugar production, held seven of the ten largest agricultural enterprises, more than ninety percent of the telephone and electric utilities and two of the three oil refineries. By 1959, U.S. investment in Cuba dominated all sectors of the economy, including public services and banking. Per capita U.S. investment in Cuba was three times higher than in the rest of Latin America.[14] These high levels of U.S. investment triggered important conflicts when the revolutionary government initiated the agrarian reform and imposed price controls on public utilities.

The Geopolitics of the Sugar Subsidy

The issue of nationalism is strongly linked with the issue of the sugar subsidy. The United States had a special policy with respect to sugar imports from Cuba. To protect domestic producers, the U.S. government established import quotas rather than imposing high tariffs on Cuban sugar imports. Consequently, sugar producers in Cuba could sell their crops to the United States at preferential prices above international levels.

Although consumers paid above-market prices for sugar, the agreement was a sweet deal for everyone else: interest groups in the United States, sugarcane producers in Cuba, U.S. investors in Cuba, and the Cuban government. The quota policy became an important geopolitical weapon for the United States to wield in the Caribbean. It was commonly used as a dissuasive instrument to manipulate political interests and to force good behavior from the Cuban government. While the Russian subsidies to the Castro regime are a well-known story, the political implication of the U.S. sugar subsidy in pre-Castro Cuba is rarely discussed. The prices paid by the United States were up to sixty percent higher than world prices.[15] Following the triumph of the revolution, the U.S. government began to threaten Cuba with the elimination of the quota. Responding to the U.S. threat, the Cuban government initiated efforts to sell sugar to other countries, including the Soviet Union. The Russians agreed to buy 425,000 tons in 1960[16] and part of the payment was made with Soviet oil. When the oil arrived in Cuba, U.S. refineries refused to process it, and the Cuban government "intervened" the refineries. The United States retaliated by suspending the sugar quota and, in November 1960, imposed an economic embargo on the island. The rest is history.

This book recounts part of that history, the ebb and flow of socialism and its impact on Cubans. Cuba's complex relationship with the United States gave the revolution a strong foothold in 1959. Nationalism and property rights helped it endure. This book looks at what has really changed in nearly forty years. Cubans negotiating in dollars, tourists on the beach, Fidel in a business suit, and the Pope delivering mass in Havana may paint a picture of a very different Cuba. But the factors that yesterday made the revolution so popular rekindle the same revolutionary zeal today.

From Batista to the Bay of Pigs
An Account of Cuba's Radicalization in 27 Months

The policy initiatives of the first months of the Cuban regime, when analyzed in their context, seem unexceptional when compared with other changes occurring throughout the region. Nevertheless, the same political agenda set in motion in Cuba a process of radicalization that was unknown in the rest of Latin America. In only twenty-seven months, Cuba's nationalistic government had traveled from the arms of the United States to the embrace of the Soviet Union. The chronology of the journey is as follows.

January 1959, the rebels enter Havana and the thesis of the Cuban revolutionary movement M-26-7 (26 of July Movement) is published. The ideological tone of the *manifesto,* very much at step with the rest of other political movements in Latin America, has the backing of the country.

February 1959, two ministries in the social arena are created: the Ministry of Social Welfare and the Ministry of Housing to initiate an aggressive housing program. That same month, the Ministry for the Recuperation of Misappropriated Goods is created to "return to the Cuban people what had been robbed by the dictator Batista and his collaborators." By this time, many of them had already fled the country. The struggle over that property continues today.

March 1959, a series of law-decrees were passed to control the prices of utilities and housing. Specifically, telephone services and later, electricity rates were fixed. These policies were consistent with the region-wide trend to subsidize prices, particularly in urban areas where newly mobilized social groups were more vocal. Leaders everywhere, from Perón in Argentina to Cárdenas in Mexico adopted price controls. In Cuba though, the fact that those services were owned and controlled by U.S. companies complicated the situation. The government could not make a decision about public utilities without stepping on U.S. interests.

April 1959, a law-decree was passed to increase the minimum wage to cane cutters. That same month, Castro went to the United States and President Eisenhower deliberately snubbed him by leaving to play golf in Georgia, (Castro had been invited to the United States by a group of newspaper editors). Richard Nixon met with Castro and described him as "incredibly naive." All these events were broadcast on Cuban television and reported in the press. Cubans consider the lack of interest on the part of the U.S. government another blow to their battered nationalism.[a]

May 1959, the Agrarian Reform Law was passed. The usual expropriation process began. No agreement was reached, especially with United Fruit, which did not accept the compensation offered by the Cuban government. The company refused the offer and tension began to mount immediately. Cuba offered twenty-year bonds at 4.5 percent interest. This offer was similar to what the Bolivian government had offered when under the agrarian reform it also expropriated land from the local landlords. Fortunately for the Bolivians, the offer was accepted, thereby avoiding further tensions.

Since the local agrarian elite was not happy either, the alliance between the Cuban landlords and U.S. investors strengthened, and both groups rested their hopes for a solution on a possible U.S. intervention. It is not until a year later, after failing to reach an agreement, that United Fruit Company farms are expropriated in April 1960.

These events (according to José Luis Rodríguez, Cuban finance minister, and referring to the agrarian reform and the confiscation of misappropriated goods) "determined a highly hostile reaction from the Cuban bourgeoisie and the U.S. imperialism acting as a block against the revolution. This increasingly hostile attitude accelerated the adoption of economic measures, which were made imperative by a class struggle that was rapidly spreading."[b]

January 1960, after negotiations failed, the United States reacted to Cuba's reformist attempts with its most important geopolitical weapon: it threatened to cut the sugar import quota.

In the context of the Cold War, Cuba reacted to the possibility of losing the U.S. sugar rent by negotiating preferential prices with the Russians. The Russians accepted the offer and in February 1960, they signed an agreement guaranteeing the trade of 425,000 tons in 1960 and one million tons per year between 1961 and 1965. Cuba was producing six million tons per year at that time.

As part of the payment for the sugar, the Soviets shipped oil to Cuba. Two of the three refineries in Cuba were U.S. property. The U.S. refineries refused to refine the oil coming from the Soviet Union. In June, the Cuban government "intervened" the Texaco refinery and forced them to refine the Russian oil.

July 1960, the United States reduced the sugar import quota by ninety-five percent in retaliation for the "intervention" of U.S. refineries. For the first time, the Cuban government had to operate without the sugar rent and the economic outlook became grim.

August 1960, Cuba retaliated with the nationalization of the most important U.S. properties in key sectors: telephone, electricity, and oil, among others. The Cuban Petroleum Institute was created.

The economic situation deteriorated rapidly. Cuban businesses with ties to the United States begin to leave. Cuba's nationalism, brewed with the unresolved racial and social tensions of the past, accelerates the radicalization process. The separation between pro-revolutionaries and anti-revolutionaries begins to divide society.

October 1960, U.S. and Cuban banks are nationalized. José Luis Rodríguez, Cuban finance minister, referred back to this event as follows "due to the open sabotage and the hostility of the Cuban upper class, the government decided to nationalize the banks (except the Canadians)."

Two Cubas were drifting apart: the upper class and ethnically white with ties to the United States versus the middle and lower classes, more ethnically black with ties to the African religion and culture. The former left; the latter stayed. In the same month, the Law for Urban Reform was passed announcing that those who left would have their assets and houses confiscated. The have-nots soon began to occupy the houses of the rich who left. The property issue in Cuba is at the core of any future reconciliation between the exiles and the Cubans in Cuba.

November 1960, the United States begins the economic embargo on Cuba.

January 1961, the government of President Dwight Eisenhower decides to break diplomatic relations with Cuba.

April 1961, a CIA-sponsored invasion force of 1,200 exiles lands at the Bay of Pigs in Cuba and is defeated within seventy-two hours. The U.S. government followed the same strategy that seven years earlier had successfully overthrown the socialist government of Arbenz in Guatemala. In Cuba, it didn't work.

Months later in 1961, Che Guevara, referring to the Bay of Pigs invasion, half jokingly said to the U.S. representative at the *Punta del Este* conference in Uruguay: "Thanks to you, we could consolidate the revolution in a particularly difficult moment."[c]

The British ambassador in Cuba informed the Foreign Office in those days:

In 1961, Fidel Castro firmly took his country to the communist sphere against the desires and instincts of its population. This was a "tour de force" that not even the prodigious Fidel Castro could have made without the disastrous invasion of April. Looked at from here the (Bay of Pigs) operation made the Suez campaign look like a successful picnic. I doubt if the prestige of the U.S. has ever been lower than after the invasion.[d]

By February 1962, an almost total embargo on Cuban trade and travel had been imposed. The embargo remains in effect.

Box Notes

a. Paterson, 1994.
b. José Luis Rodríguez, *Estrategia del Desarrollo Economico en Cuba.*
c. Jorge Castañeda, 254.
d. British Embassy, Havana to the Earl Home, January 11, 1962. Foreign Office Archive, London. FO 371/62308, Ref. 9843, p.5 in Jorge Castañeda, 254.

Notes

1. Pope John Paul II, Speech on his visit to Havana, Cuba, January 21, 1998.
2. The *milicianos* were militiamen, or armed forces of the revolution.
3. Mesa-Lago, *The Economy of Socialist Cuba*.
4. Gerchunoff, "Peronist Economic Policies, 1946–1955."
5. Hilliker, *The Politics of Reform in Peru*.
6. Szulc, *Fidel: A Critical Portrait*.
7. Castañeda, *La Vida en Rojo*.
8. Schlesinger, *Bitter Fruit*.
9. *See* Kline, "Cuba: the Politics of Socialist Revolution" in Wiarda and Kline, eds., *Latin American Politics and Development*.
10. Cole Blasier, "The United States and the Revolution" in Malloy, ed., *Beyond the Revolution*.
11. The U.S., not Spain, was the dominant economic power on the island. *See* Cardoso and Helwege, *Cuba After Communism*.
12. The Guantanamo Naval Base, still a source of conflict between the U.S. and Cuba, was set up under the stipulations of this treaty.
13. The radio used by the revolutionary movement from the Sierra Maestra.
14. Kline, "Cuba: The Politics of Socialist Revolution."
15. Kline, "Cuba: The Politics of Socialist Revolution."
16. Cuba's total production was six million tons.

2

LIVING WITH SOCIALISM

> The great society is a place where men are more con-
> cerned about the quality of their goals than the quantity
> of their goods.
>
> Lyndon B. Johnson, 1964[1]

By 1970 it was clear that Cuba was a socialist state. In fact, Cubans were living smack dab in the middle of socialism's heyday on the island. The government had yet to compromise on basic socialist principles and people had learned to live within that system.

Amparo was a product of the revolution, and most of the time she believed in it. But believing didn't mean her life was easy. Her life was full of trade-offs that were decided more by the government than by herself. Before analyzing Cuba's economic reforms, it is important to try and understand the baseline: socialism. What was it like to live in socialism? What was it like to live in Cuba in the early 1970s? In trying to answer these questions, this chapter does not simply describe the socialist rules of the game; it looks at how Amparo, a Cuban economist in 1970, lived by these rules.

Amparo was making the morning coffee for herself and her husband Jaime when the bad news came over the radio. The voice from the small 1956 General Electric receiver was loud and strong. Despite much hard work by thousands of farmers and volunteers from schools and factories, the sugar harvest had fallen short of the ten-million-ton target for 1970. More than 1.2 million people, out of a total population of 8.6 million, from various sectors of the economy were mobilized to work the sugar fields in order to compensate for the lack of capital and mechanical support for the sugar harvest. The investment plan for the sector was not carried out on time and the machinery was not available for the harvest. It was a deep disappointment. "Sugar is not the problem," she thought, sipping her sweet coffee. The *libreta* (rationing card) always allows for enough sugar—a full ten pounds a month. But what about everything else, all the things Cuba trades in exchange for sugar[2] with other countries—especially the U.S.S.R. Food, clothes, shoes and coffee!!! She swallowed hard on the last gulp of this precious commodity as she realized that their three-quarters-of-a-pound monthly ration was almost gone. And with the economy on the downslide, their rationing card would probably be right in its wake.

Clarita, her cousin, was coming to visit from Venezuela and she had to be prepared. She had warned Clarita many times not to send money in the mail; now, she asked her not to bring dollars with her. It was illegal to carry dollars and trading in the black market was done principally in pesos. She preferred to live by the rules. She made a mental checklist of the goods she'd be allotted on her *libreta* next month: besides the ten pounds of sugar and the three-quarters of a pound of coffee, she could count on five ounces of beans, twelve ounces of meat, and twenty pounds of rice. She paused for a moment and wondered whether she'd get eggs this time. It would be nice to offer Clarita eggs for breakfast; that's the least she could do for someone coming from such a rich country. She continued ticking off her mental list. Toothpaste, bathroom and laundry soap, toilet paper, one liter of cooking oil, one pack of cigarettes. If they saved up on toilet paper and soap and picked up a few things in the black market, they'd be all set to receive their guest. She remembered that Jaime had a pair of eyeglasses from last year's quota. Since he didn't need them, they might be able to exchange them for some more food for Clarita's visit.

Cuba's black market was alive and well in those days, it just wasn't dollarized like it is today. The products in the black market came either from stolen goods at the workplace or unwanted items from the *libreta*. Last month, Amparo had traded a pair of shoes that didn't fit, for a dress which didn't fit somebody else. Fashion and good looks were obviously not a revolutionary concern. On the contrary, any criticism of the limited choice or bad quality of clothes was considered anti-revolutionary and selfish.

Amparo was an economist, and she pondered her country's recent economic history with sadness. Every year since 1966, Cuba had missed its sugar production target. But in 1970, the last year of the five-year plan, hopes were high that the goal would finally be reached. Raising sugar production had become a particularly daunting task in the face of the revolutionary government's new agricultural strategy of diversification. In 1961, after criticizing the country's over-dependence on sugar, the government decided to diversify into a variety of agricultural products regardless of its costs.

Table 2.1   Sugar Production: A Goal Never Achieved (millions of tons)

	1966	1967	1968	1969	1970
Production (plan)	6.5	7.5	8.0	9.0	10.0
Production (real)	4.9	6.2	5.3	5.5	7.6
Difference	–1.6	–1.3	–2.7	–3.5	–2.4
Export USSR (plan)	3.1	4.0	5.0	5.0	5.0
Export USSR (real)	2.2	2.5	1.7	1.3	3.0
Difference	–0.8	–1.5	–3.3	–3.7	–2.0

Source: Estrategia de Desarrollo Económico en Cuba. José Luis Rodriguez. Editorial de Ciencias Sociales, La Habana, Cuba, 1990, 122.

The strategy turned out to be a mistake, and by 1964, Che Guevara had admitted the failure. "Shifting the use of land from sugar to other agricultural products had been a fundamental error," he confessed, because they had misinterpreted the concept of diversification:

> Instead of going ahead with the process in relative terms, we did it in absolute terms. Simultaneously, this produced an over-dispersion of resources in a large number of agricultural sectors which we erroneously tended to justify in the name of diversification.[3]
>
> The mistake we made in the agricultural sector during 1960 and 1961 was two-fold: first, we relegated sugar cane as if we needed to do so in order to diversify. Second, we took diversification to the local extreme by converting every farm into a mosaic of crops.[4]

Diversification became a question of security rather than economics. The goal was economic independence, at all cost, regardless of whether or not it made economic sense. Little attention was paid to whether Cuba could be competitive in other crops. The rule of thumb appeared to be, if you eat it, grow it.

The other major problem was that diversification was applied to everyone, and anyone. Not only were large commercial farms forced to diversify, but even small farms had to divide up their production into mini-plots that had no economic reason for being.

Despite its many mistakes, there was no doubt in Amparo's mind: the Revolution was the best thing that could have happened to her. Unlike her parents, she had a university degree that cost her nothing; so did her husband. They had a beautiful son, whom she could drop off on her way to work at an excellent day care center—for free. Her son's education and health care would be freely provided for by the state forever. Not only had these social services provided her with personal peace of mind, but they had also paid off nationally with a healthier, better educated population. The infant mortality rate per 1,000 births had been reduced from 60 in 1958 to 35.9 in 1970. And the percentage of the population with a sixth-grade education or more, had increased from 20.1 percent to 31.6 percent over the same period.

Her parents had plenty of worries at her age that she had been spared. She almost died of meningitis when she was only a year old. In those days, good health care was private; so was good education. Her parents were getting older, but with the new pension system and universally free health care, she didn't have to worry about that either. If Cuba could only raise sugar production, everything would be fine. Fidel had put it very clearly: "With our sugar we can have the hard currency. It is there (in sugar production) where we can get the foreign exchange and the resources for the development of our industry."[5]

By 1964, Fidel had proposed a change in the economic strategy, putting the emphasis on boosting sugar production from 4.6 million to 10 million tons.

If the 1965–1970 plan failed, they would come up with something else, thought Amparo, who had great faith in the government's ability to come up with a workable economic plan. What her degree in Marxist economics hadn't explained to her was that in a market economy, most of the difficult decisions that challenged Cuban policymakers' ideological commitment are made automatically by a multiplicity of private investors. She still believed that a small group of well-intentioned policymakers could come up with *The Plan* for sustainable growth and social welfare. She had never read the English jurist Albert Dicey who fifty years earlier had warned his readers about this dangerous belief by describing socialism as: "the government for the good of the people, by experts or officials who know—or think they know—what is good for the people, better than any non-official person, or than the mass of the people themselves."[6]

With her confidence in the country leadership, she had more immediate concerns: getting her son dressed, finishing breakfast and coffee—oh yes, the coffee. She had lost her train of thought. She turned to her husband and suggested he get in touch with their "red market" contact, Marino. "We are running out of coffee and our next ration isn't due for two weeks. Tell him we have a bottle of rum *Añejo* to trade for coffee with the Russians. But be firm with him. You know how these Russians are. They think we're all stupid. We want at least three

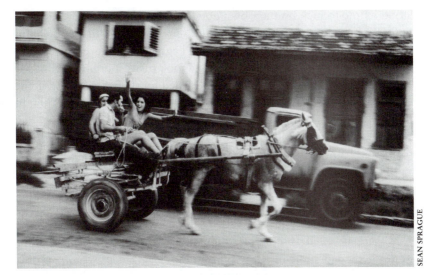

SEAN SPRAGUE

She'll get where she's going . . . the Cuban way.

pounds of coffee for that bottle. If not, we can get a better deal some-where else in the black market."

The red markets were where Soviets stationed in Cuba bought goods from their special stores and resold them to Cubans. The islanders paid for these goods in pesos or in rum. Most of the time, the rum came from illegally processed sugarcane in the countryside. The Soviets lived a sepa-rate existence in Cuba. They didn't like to mix with the locals, and the locals felt the same way. In the red market, a few Cubans and Russians essentially met for the sole purpose of exchanging products. The Rus-sians had their own neighborhoods with their own dollar stores, their own schools, and even their own beaches. Although Cubans resented this, they realized the Russian presence was vital for survival. On a macro level, the Russians were paying inflated prices for Cuban sugar exports. On a micro level, the red market, where Russians traded im-ported products for rum and cigars, made life for Cubans more tolerable.

All clothing was also made available through the *libreta*. Jaime, for instance, received a pair each of dress pants and work pants every six months, plus three corduroy or denim shirts. Annually, he received a pair of good leather shoes and a few pairs of socks. To collect their rationed goods, people had to endure long lines and, not surprisingly, they often complained. For many people, their job was to stand in line for others who were employed and could not spend hours waiting. Amparo, always looking on the bright side, thought this was a great opportunity for housewives to make a little extra money while they stood in line to pick up their own goods. It reminded her of when they got their bicycle. A friend working in a state store told them of a shipment that was about to arrive. The line began to form even before the bicycles had arrived. Amparo and Jaime took turns standing on line for four days, but they were eventually rewarded for their patience with the treasured bike. She felt sorry for those who stayed in line for nothing, but she was sure their turn would come someday. Last month, they were relieved to make the final payment for the bike with a ten-peso deduction from her payroll. Finally, the bicycle was theirs.

In a socialist economy, people have few choices, and in Cuba, it was no different. Houses were assigned and could not be sold; schools were designated; the amount of food a family could eat was decided centrally and apportioned by the *libreta,* as were clothing and shoes. Jobs were assigned and people could choose their careers only if they performed adequately in school; if not, the government would encourage the student to pursue something else.

No wonder when Clarita landed at José Martí Airport in Havana she was fascinated by what she saw. She thought she had just emerged from a time tunnel. The cars parked outside the airport were all from the 1950s. Compared to Caracas, there was very little traffic, but the streets were swarming with people. The architecture of the city was stunning and the old buildings were wonderful. Clarita couldn't think of another city in Latin America with such a generalized, classical beauty. Colonial mansions once owned by the very rich were now the home of many. The other homes, however, were too small, and the heat too intense to stay inside the non–air-conditioned houses.

As the taxi made its way from the airport to her cousin's house, Clarita contemplated the city in the growing darkness. It was different from any other city she had ever seen, not for something unique that was there, but for things that were noticeably absent. There were no neon lights, no billboards, no stores, no "Drink Coca Cola" or "Fly Pan Am" signs; just walls painted with "socialism or death."

Brainwashed by movies that typified people in socialist societies as gloomy, reserved, and bored, Clarita was pleasantly surprised by Cubans and their warm, open attitude. They had a great sense of humor, making jokes about the little tragedies of daily life. They were optimistic and friendly, and above all, Cubans were then, as they are today, very proud people. Coming from another country in Latin America—the continent with the highest social inequality in the world—Clarita was particularly impressed with the intended fairness of the Cuban system. In Venezuela, she had gone to a private school and a private university; her daughter

SEAN SPRAGUE

Even the wear and tear of revolution neglect cannot diminish the splendor of Havana.

was born in a private hospital; nobody she knew would dare use the public health system. She and her husband had two cars and had never used public transportation. But she had two maids who told her how difficult life was for them and their children. Their stories made Clarita feel guilty and very sorry for those less fortunate than she.

So Cuba was a breath of fresh air for her; social equality and solidarity were ideas that made her feel comfortable. For the first time, she could walk the streets and feel just like everyone else. She felt at ease walking with Amparo to go buy bread. The store was three blocks away and they chatted while standing in line. After almost an hour's wait, they finally got the bread. It was cold and hard, but Amparo didn't seem to notice. Clarita very definitely did. "This bread is awful. How can you eat this thing, especially in the morning? Don't they have anything else?" she asked naively. People turned to look at her, and many answered for Amparo. What was she talking about? Where was she from? What kind of comment was that? Didn't she know?"

Then, as now, there were few private conversations in Cuba. Conversations were a public good; everybody felt entitled to jump in and participate in any exchange of ideas. It was fun, but it helped Clarita begin to understand that equality and freedom are a very difficult combination to achieve simultaneously. The trade-off between freedom and equality continues to be a big question for societies—not the least of which is Cuba; and as many have learned, the answer is neither simple nor easy.

Notes

1. Lyndon B. Johnson, Speech at the University of Michigan, May 22, 1964. http://www.famousquotes.com
2. Cuba's foreign trade had become highly concentrated with socialist economies. From 1960 to 1963, trade with the socialist world had grown from 21.6 percent to 75.8 percent of total trade. By 1963, the Soviet Union had become Cuba's single most important trading partner, accounting for 44.3 percent of its foreign trade. *See* José Luis Rodríguez, *Estrategia del Desarrollo Economico en Cuba,* 104.
3. Ernesto Guevara, "Cuba: su economía, su comercio exterior, su significación en el mundo actual," *Nuestra Industria Económica,* no. 10, in José Luis Rodríguez, *Estrategia del Desarrollo Economico en Cuba.*
4. Carlos Rodríguez, "El Nuevo Camino."
5. Fidel Castro, Speech at the VI anniversary of the triumph of the Revolution, January 1965.
6. A.V. Dicey, "Introduction to the Study of the law of the Constitution," 1914. Taken from Robert Skidelsky, *The Road from Serfdom* (London: Penguin Books, 1995), 17.

3

SOCIALISM OR GROWTH:

CUBA IN THE GOLDEN '80S

> The mistake with the most pernicious consequences
> was the belief that only economic mechanisms would
> insure the construction of socialism.
>
> Fidel Castro, 1986[1]

Socialism or death! That is the most distinctive slogan of revolutionary Cuba. For nearly four decades, all speeches denouncing both external and internal threats to socialist ideology have ended with this familiar outcry. "Socialism or death!" respond the masses in collective cathar-sis, gathering strength to fight the enemy—whoever and wherever it may be.

The history of the Cuban revolution is awash with examples of obvious external threats: the U.S. embargo, the Bay of Pigs, the haphazard relationship with the Soviet Union, and the recent downfall of socialism in Eastern Europe. As menacing as these external threats may have seemed, they have been easier and less costly to overcome than Cubans' own unwitting affronts to their socialist ideals: the natural human drive of self-interest and individualism. Reflecting this tension, the island has flirted with capitalism since the revolution and has seemed to alternately embrace and reject limited economic openings throughout the socialist period. The result: a perennial, politically charged balancing act between the drive for efficiency and loyalty to socialist principles. Freedom versus equality has been the ever-present political trade-off in Cuba's revolutionary history. But the socialist utopia has been conspiring constantly against economic efficiency and growth. "Socialism or growth" would seem to be the economic counterpart to the famous political slogan. When market incentives have been implemented the economy has grown and inevitably, some people have been left behind. For an egalitarian society like Cuba's, the choice between socialism and

27

growth has, to date, been easy: socialism has always won out. The reforms of the late 1970s and early 1980s are a good example. For most Cubans, those were the best years of the revolution.

After the poor economic showing of the early 1970s, Cuba initiated a series of market-oriented reforms that set the stage for a flourishing period in the 1980s. Free farmers' markets, material incentives, and managerial independence for state enterprises were some of these reforms. Ironically, while the economy was booming and productivity was increasing, the leadership decided to look back and take refuge in socialist ideals. José Luis Rodríguez, current Finance Minister of Cuba, refers to the experience of the 1980s this way: "In socialism, an adequate economic policy must make social interest prevail over private interest and moral incentives over material ones."[2]

Why did Cuba decide to relax its socialist principles in the first place? What motivated Cuban leaders to tip the political balance?

Living in the '80s

Julio pushed his way through the crowded bus from Miramar to downtown Havana. The University had finally paid him the bonus and he decided to buy some delicacies at the former Sears store, now *Tienda La Amistad*. It was December, 1985, and his wife, six months pregnant, had a craving for fruit yogurt and chocolate cake. "Whoever invented cravings wasn't a socialist. How did women manage fifteen years ago? You can't exactly buy a banquet with a rationing card," commented Julio to his friend Pedro, manager of one of the most successful companies in Havana.

Pedro wasn't paying much attention. He was really excited; his soaps and perfumes were a hit and sales had been increasing steadily. After launching five new product lines, profits were skyrocketing. Bonuses were going to be hefty this December; perfect timing for a good New Year's party.

The 1980s were good years for more than just consumers. For managers, they were times of prosperity, excitement, and choice. For the first time since the nationalizations of 1961, companies were free to make at least some decisions: basically, a little bit of product design and marketing. Productivity incentives were also introduced: workers and managers could as much as double their basic salary if they substantially increased their productivity.

This was a big change from the 1960s, when Che Guevara had helped define Cuba's two most important economic objectives: self-sufficiency in agricultural products and accelerated industrialization. When he was named Minister of Basic Industries in 1962, he decided to eliminate individual company decisions by grouping nationalized companies in sectors with centralized management and a consolidated budget. The general manager of Suchel, a successfully decentralized company in today's Cuba, remembered how things worked back then. "General managers were just production supervisors. In our sector, there were fifty or sixty companies, Colgate and Procter among others. Managers had very little freedom; product lines were minimal, goods were only produced for *la libreta,* the type and quantity (quotas) were centrally planned. Basically, we worked very hard all the time to meet the quotas assigned to us."

But the '80s were different. Julio's wife, Albita, was fortunate to be pregnant in a very different era. Flourishing trade with the socialist bloc and market-oriented reforms had vastly improved life for Cubans. Fruit yogurt with buffalo milk and Copellia, the best ice cream in Cuba, were sold in food stores; shrimp, crabs, chocolates, Polish pickles, cold cuts, cakes, perfumed soap, and shampoo were among the large variety of products available in pesos at the *Amistad* stores. Julio was a university professor. He was making 320 pesos a month and his wife made 280. With the bonus system, he managed to make another 400 pesos by teaching a few more hours a week. Material[3] incentives had also been implemented in the universities. Bonuses were being used to increase productivity and it was working. With a family income of 1,000 pesos, 55 pesos for the *libreta,* another 100 pesos for rent and transportation, they lived well. And under the new real estate law, they could finally buy the apartment they had been living in for the past six years.

Ten years later, the same couple would be earning a salary only fifteen percent higher—without bonuses—while food would be twenty times more expensive. But in those days, Julio was optimistic about the future; he had no reason not to be. The economy was in great shape. As a matter of fact, he had just read the five-year economic report for 1980–85 published by the Banco Nacional de Cuba. Growth had averaged 7.3 percent[4] annually, which was double the growth rate of the previous five-year period. The efficiency gains resulting from changes in the System of Economic Management and Planning (SDPE) as well as high investment ratios in the 1976–1980 period had boosted Cuba's economic performance in the first half of the 1980s. Moreover, the consolidation of the trade agreement with the Soviet Bloc had oriented investment and production into areas where Cuba had a competitive advantage. He was an economist; he had reason to believe that things

TABLE 3.1   A Booming Economy: Selected Data

	1980–1985
Total average growth	7.3%
Industry	6.9%
Construction	8.6%
Transportation	6.4%
Communication	9.6%
Sugar	1.7%
Non-sugar agriculture	3.8%

Source: Banco Nacional de Cuba, CEE, La Habana, Cuba, 1985.

were changing for the better. His wife was not. She was a politician, an active member of the Party, and she could see problems coming.

Why? What was wrong? Why all the criticism? After all, the figures looked great.

The economy's performance during the 1980–85 period was being evaluated in preparation for the III Party Congress in 1986. Albita had been in on the discussions. More than 400,000 people participated in almost 20,000 meetings in all the provinces. The debate was widespread. The new economic strategy was under fire. Creeping inequality and widespread corruption were being denounced and criticized. What changes had been made and why the criticism?

"Sugar-coated" Socialism

For more than a decade, revolutionary Cuba followed an economic strategy based on overdiversification and self-sufficiency. By the late 1970s, this misguided strategy coupled with the constraints of the U.S. embargo had resulted in continuous food shortages, production bottlenecks, and growing inefficiencies throughout the economy. Fidel was losing confidence in his policymakers, who in turn were losing confidence in socialism.

Motivated in large part by the need to overcome its economic problems, Cuba turned to the protective arms of the Soviet Union. After joining the Council of Mutual Economic Assistance (CMEA), the Soviet bloc trade alliance, socialism became decidedly more palatable for

TABLE 3.2   Average Sugar Prices Per Pound:
The Soviets Paid Three Times the International Prices

	1975–1979
International	11.5 cents
Paid by the CMEA	36.4 cents

Source: Torres, Olga, *"El Desarrollo de la Economía Cubana a partir de 1959"* in Revista Comercio Exterior 31, no. 3, Mexico, 1981.

most Cubans. With little more than the island's sugar production, it was able to trade with its socialist cohorts for a wide range of goods. But that was only the first course in its expanded economic menu. Cuba also implemented a series of economic and administrative changes that added a taste of capitalism to the system. It was the island's version of the pre-Gorbachev era.

The decision to join the CMEA was a sweet deal indeed. Cuba was charged with supplying the Soviet bloc with sugar, nickel, cobalt, rum, and citrus while the Soviets provided most of the rest. No more worries about self-sufficiency or heavy industrialization. Deals were mainly made through barter agreements, in which Cuba would ship sugar at subsidized prices, nickel, and refined oil in exchange for foodstuffs, industrial equipment, and consumer goods. Among the agreements signed between Cuba and the Soviet Union were: a) to produce 30,000 tons of nickel and cobalt, b) to invest $1.4 billion in the production of citrus, and c) to trade sugar for refined oil at pre-set fixed prices.

All these agreements were measured in transferable rubles, a currency which was non-convertible outside the Soviet bloc. Thanks to the CMEA, Cuba also benefited from compensatory mechanisms for import price increases, preferential long-term credits, preferential rates for technical assistance and fuel re-exports in convertible currency. With all this comfortable protection and increasing Soviet dependency, up to eighty-seven percent of Cuba's foreign trade was with the CMEA, the highest concentration of all CMEA members.

For some, Cuba's incorporation in the CMEA reflected an ideological coincidence with a most predictable outcome: very close ties and cooperation. For others it was "the only alternative to the blockade imposed by the United States on Cuba since the first years of the Revolution."[5] Whatever the causes—probably a combination of both ideological compatibility and economic desperation—the results were dramatic: the Sovietization of the Cuban economy. At the same time, however, a few decidedly capitalist threads were being woven through Cuba's socialist economic fabric.

A Little Slack for State Enterprises

Some market-oriented adjustments similar to the pre-Gorbachev era were introduced under the System of Economic Management and Planning (SDPE).[6] The objective was to impose budgetary discipline while giving state enterprises more managerial independence. For example, the new system allowed companies to engage in market transactions. Products and services were priced and inter-enterprise transactions were not only accounted for in volumes, but also in sales income. Thus, companies were allowed to buy and sell at set prices, to have their own accounting system and also to keep their own profit accounts. These profit accounts were a profound innovation for the traditional centrally planned budgets. Since the accounting system was decentralized, companies could, for the first time, evaluate their performance and decide how to reduce costs and increase profits. Although prices were centrally set, managers could still make other decisions regarding volumes and product lines after complying with the centrally planned quota. Soon they began to make decisions such as reallocating resources to increase profits: cost cutting, concentration on profitable lines, productivity bonuses, independent decisions, choice, large wage differentials. Soon some eyebrows began to rise. Castro summarized the sentiment with the following statement:

> With the system called SDPE we are supposedly trying to increase economic efficiency and labor productivity. Now, there is no system in socialism by which you can substitute politics, ideology and people's conscience. The factors that have determined efficiency in a capitalist economy are others. They cannot exist in socialism where the political, ideological and moral aspects are still fundamental factors in the system.

Free Farmers' Markets: Relieving the Bottlenecks

Since the revolution in 1959, the agricultural sector has been at the forefront of most economic activity not entirely dictated by the socialist model. Indeed, private farms have existed throughout the history of modern Cuba. The 1959 Agrarian Reform Law created small private farms on approximately sixty-five percent of the land. Many of the farmers who received land were sharecroppers and tenant farmers before

SEAN SPRAGUE

In 1985 Cubans rushed to markets before the government closed them down.

the revolution. These farms number about 102,000 and range in size from twenty to sixty hectares. Until 1980, the private farmers sold their products to the government, which controlled the distribution, wholesale, and retail of the goods. In 1986, approximately seven percent of arable land in Cuba was in private hands, thirteen percent was owned by cooperatives, and eighty percent was government land. The private farms have had consistently higher productivity rates than the government-run farms, even though they generally have less access to fertilizers and machinery.

By the end of the '70s, Cuba's centralized system and its attendant inefficiencies had prevented the agricultural sector from meeting its production goals. Input shortages had become rampant and were aggravated by hoarding in response to uncertain supply.[7] To alleviate food shortages, the government announced in the spring of 1980 Decree 66 legalizing free farmers' markets, or *mercados libres campesinos* (MLCs). By the middle of the decade, 250 such MLCs had been established. Private farmers were allowed to sell their products at the MLCs at free prices, provided they first met quotas for sales to the government. The MLCs undercut the black market and alleviated some shortages. Cubans flocked to the markets and enjoyed the greater variety that was available, though complaints of high prices were common. Fish, chicken, rabbit, and lamb (beef was still controlled by a state monopoly) and vegetables and fruit became more readily available to Cuban consumers almost overnight.

The government had hoped to improve the productivity of state-run farms and be able to undersell private farmers if their prices climbed too high. Private Cuban farmers, however, proved adept at working this small capitalist opening to their advantage. They closely monitored what the state stores were offering and then brought to the free markets goods they knew were not available from the government. The ensuing seller's market drove prices up and led to allegations of widespread corruption. In 1982 government investigators cracked down on the markets, arresting 165 people for "irregularities," including involvement of middlemen in the markets and the sale of products stolen from the government. The Cuban commerce minister at the time, Manuel Vila Sosa, claimed that sixty percent of the goods sold at the MLCs had been stolen from the government. After the crackdown, government controls were imposed on these markets, including a twenty percent sales tax and a progressive income tax ranging from five to twenty percent. Despite the stricter controls, the markets continued to thrive.

The reaction was not good and criticism became widespread:

> The incentive mechanisms in the free farmers' markets were full of errors. In fact we have created an uncontrolled source of mercantile income. The worst effect—more than economic—is political since it favors illicit enrichment and the resurfacing of bourgeois ideas. (Granma, July 1986)

Wage Incentives

Some initiatives date back to the earliest days of Cuba's socialist history. Even in the 1960s under Minister of Industry Che Guevara, a committed Marxist, workers were paid 0.5 percent of their wage for every one percent of overproduction achieved. The record of wage incentives in Cuba reflects the general pattern that capitalist reforms have followed in the country: they were adopted, then disavowed when they began to undermine socialist ideals, then adopted again when economic realities demanded it. In 1967, the leadership believed they had achieved a "communist consciousness" which rendered wage incentives unnecessary; they were abandoned. The resulting decline in productivity and standards of living inspired a policy reversal.

The existence of wage incentives in the Cuban economy was codified with the General Reform of 1980. The Reform raised the average wage by 4.5 percent and firmly established the connection between wages earned and the quantity and quality of work done by individuals. The prices of certain products that had been frozen since 1962, despite rising input costs, were hiked. The results of the Reform were dramatic: labor productivity leaped ten percent in 1981 while the average productivity increase for the 1980–1985 period was four percent.

In spite of all these achievements, criticism abounded:

> The economist tendency which pretends to promote the achievement of production goals by only calling on material rewards, does not promote a satisfactory working behavior, quite the opposite it enthrones indiscipline and insubordination. (Granma, July 1986)

Self-employment: More Jobs and More Services

Another free market reform during this period was the state's 1978 decision to allow limited self-employment. Certain professionals such as carpenters, plumbers, electricians, and artisans were allowed to work privately, provided they had first fulfilled their time commitment to the state. Those who were able to buy a state license could essentially go into business for themselves. They charged whatever rate they could get, and payment was often made in kind with goods such as chickens or vegetables. They were not allowed to hire any staff, but they could form business alliances with colleagues.

The 1978 legalization of self-employment was considered an attempt to control what had been occurring for quite some time. Artisans and handymen had seemingly always worked outside the state apparatus, risking detention by the authorities as they attempted to improve their standard of living. Even after the 1978 reforms such work was a potentially dangerous proposition. The state strictly controlled the number of licenses issued for private work, and crackdowns such as the trial of a score of artisans in a public square in Santiago de Cuba in June, 1985, for selling jewelry without a license were common.

Foreign Investment Reform: Looking for New Partners

Another significant development in Cuba that anticipated the market reforms of the 1990s was the passage of Law-Decree 50 in 1982. This law allows foreigners to own up to forty-nine percent of local businesses. It also allows foreigners to control labor, pricing, and production policies, and to repatriate profits. The law was structured to compel international investors to bear more risk than if finance capital were invested. Negotiations for some investment projects with Canadian and West European companies were initiated after Law-Decree 50 came into effect, but pressure from the Reagan administration on potential investors limited the benefits of the law. Law-Decree 50 was the base upon which the current foreign investment climate was created; in 1992 it was expanded and became a cornerstone of Cuban economic policy.

Real Estate Reform

In the early 1980s, the Cuban government relaxed previous restrictions on construction materials and in 1984 enacted a new housing law. This law allowed all present and future tenants to buy their homes by converting their leases with the state into long-term sales contracts with monthly mortgage payments in the same amount as the rent they previously paid. According to official estimates, by 1986 close to 500,000 deeds had been turned in to comply with the law. The liberalization of the housing and construction materials markets created a housing boom in the first half of the 1980s. Housing construction rates reached their highest point since the revolution. According to official sources, 153,646 homes were built from 1980 to 1984, nearly twice the number constructed from 1975 to 1979. Private housing construction accounted for thirty-four percent during the same period.[8]

The introduction of free farmers' markets, artisan markets, and a housing market improved efficiency and fostered national income growth. Resource allocation became more efficient as market incentives were introduced to different sectors of the economy. Labor productivity also increased an average 3.7 percent per year. Of course, the aid provided by the former Soviet Union was an important factor in the economic success of the early 1980s. Nonmilitary assistance from the USSR nearly quadrupled from 1974 to 1979 when it reached $3 billion, about one quarter of Cuban GDP for the same year.[9]

The Rectification: Ideology over Economics

> Together with the errors of the SDPE there was the stupid belief that the economic mechanisms were going to do the job of the party, that those mechanisms were going to build socialism and that those mechanisms were going to bring development.
>
> Also the Party is to blame, it neglected the economic problems, leaving them only to the experts.
>
> Fidel Castro, 1986

By 1986, the reforms had generated considerable tension in Cuban politics and society. The MLCs and the liberalized construction materials market, for example, diverted valuable resources from state to private uses. The MLCs had brought with them the specter of the much-hated "middleman," truckers who would "exploit" the free farmers' lack of transportation by buying produce cheaply in the countryside, bringing it to the cities, and selling it at a hefty profit. Income differentials were becoming more obvious to Cuban citizens, as truck drivers typically earned many times more than physicians. Housing law reforms unleashed a speculative boom in real estate, and prices shot up. Government officials were concerned that the reforms might exact a toll on the people's socialist fervor and award a few select beneficiaries undue influence. At the same time, however, the government fully realized the positive economic impact of liberalization. Indeed, the need for further decentralization had been extolled in various government documents and speeches in the months prior to the 1986 Third Congress of the Cuban Communist Party, particularly at the 1985 Fourth Plenary session.

At the Third Party Congress, many a heated discussion focused on the future direction of the economy. The role of material incentives in a socialist system was once again the subject of fierce debate in Cuba. The lack of foreign exchange stalled the impetus for further changes as the government tried to marshal all available resources to complete several long-term investment projects. The result was a period known as the Rectification Process, which aimed to renew socialism and rejected many of the capitalistic openings of the late 1970s and early 1980s.

Clearly, the government's about-face was very politically and ideologically inspired. Volunteerism was revived with the resurrection of "micro-brigades" of unemployed and temporarily laid off workers, originally a Guevara innovation. Castro, who visited North Korea in 1986 and was impressed by that country's hard line Communism, invoked a more virulent anti-capitalist tone reminiscent of the early days of the revolutionary period.

Decrying what he called the "thousands of wheeler-dealers who cheat, sell and steal," Castro summarily closed the MLCs on May 15, 1986. At a meeting of four thousand representatives of Cuba's farm cooperatives two days before the announcement of the shutdown, Castro let on that the decision to "rectify" had already been made: "Our fight against these neo-capitalists that have arisen will not be limited to the elimination of the free farmers' markets: we are going to fight against these tendencies and manifestations on all fronts and in all places."

He went on to say that: "In the search for economic efficiency, we have created a culture for a heap of evils and deformation, and what is worse, corruption . . . . It is a moral issue, one of principle and dignity not to surrender to commercialism and speculation."

The six-year experiment in free enterprise had grown to be a serious irritant for the regime, so much so that it was willing to sacrifice

$83 million worth of produce sold to the public annually by the MLCs. The resulting food scarcity was exacerbated when private forms of transportation were suddenly removed and up to thirty-five percent of certain crops rotted in the fields.[10]

Other free-market openings were abandoned as well. The 1984 housing law was amended to give more control to the state and halt the speculation that had arisen. All housing sales had to be approved by a state agency that would also regulate prices. And the government again began to exercise its legal right to buy all housing for sale on the market.

In 1986, Castro also labeled the thousands of self-employed Cubans "corrupt parasites" on the public sector and curbed their activities with tighter regulations. In an effort to gain greater control over resources, the government imposed a system in which taxi drivers, artisans, street vendors, and private service workers such as plumbers and electricians had to obtain all materials via a state-issued certificate. The number of private wage and self-employed workers fell from 52,100 in 1985 to 43,200 in 1987. In monetary terms, private non-farm incomes fell from 102.5 million pesos to 67.8 million pesos in the same period. During the Rectification Period, wage incentives for the population were also scaled back.

The Shock

Cubans watched the fall of the Soviet Union in 1989 with stupefaction, disbelief, and panic. It had happened again, first with the United States and now with the Soviet Union. "We will never let this happen to us for the third time, we have learned the lesson, from now on we don't want marriages, we want as many partners as possible" said Marcos Portal, Minister for Heavy Industry in 1995.

Without the massive Soviet subsidies, life was unimaginable for Cubans. More than ninety percent of the island's oil consumption was supplied by the Soviets. Oil shipments from the U.S.S.R. to Cuba averaged thirteen million tons by 1989, more than twice as much as total 1995 oil imports. The Castro government had sold excess oil on the world market to earn sorely needed hard currency. These re-exports during the 1980s provided between four and ten percent of Cuba's total exports.

The harsh reality began to sink in. Cuba's foreign trade had become dangerously concentrated; over eighty-four percent of total external commerce was with the Soviet bloc.[11] And now that bloc was crumbling. By

1989, one hundred percent of Cuba's bread was made with Soviet wheat, sixty-five percent of the powdered milk came from the Soviets, as did fifty percent of its fertilizers and forty percent of its rice. From sugar mills and oil refineries to cars, buses, televisions, and refrigerators, everything was dependent on spare parts from the CMEA countries. Cubans were shocked when Gorbachev told Castro there would be no more sugar price supports; Cuba would be paid the international market price for its sugar and its agriculture minister would have to buy and sell all agricultural commodities. Cubans were dumbfounded when the Hungarians presented them with an ultimatum: pay, *in dollars,* twenty percent more for the Ikarus buses assembled on the island, or consider the contract terminated.[12] Also it was a shock for Cubans to find out that the central planning agency was no longer in charge of the trade operations of Russian companies. Cuban government officials were perplexed when after inquiring at the Gosplan office in Moscow about their annual shipment of home refrigerators, they were sent to negotiate directly with the plant managers in the city of Minsk. Perhaps the greatest shock was when thousands of Russian technicians and military aids simply packed their bags and left. Then, in 1991, Russia asked the West to include sugar in its food aid.

Trade with the Soviet bloc was disintegrating and Cuba had nowhere to turn. There was virtually no foreign investment from non-Soviet countries in spite of the 1982 Investment Law's intent to attract new partners. Cuba was not—and is still not—a member of the International Monetary Fund, the Inter-American Development Bank, or the World Bank. Aid to Cuba from these banks was out of the question, while the countries of the former Soviet Union became the darlings of these institutions. The U.S. embargo was the *coup de grace* for Cuba's trade relations with the rest of the world.

That was the situation in 1989. Cuba was at the brink of collapse and the whole world was watching. The slogans, the political and economic choices of revolutionary Cuba had taken on new meaning: socialism or death, socialism or growth, socialism or survival. What were the alternatives?

Notes

1. Fidel Castro, Interview with Jeffrey Elliot and Mervin M. Demally, March 29, 1985, in José Luis Rodriguez, *Estrategia del Desarrollo Económico en Cuba.*
2. José Luis Rodríguez, *Estrategia del Desarrollo Económico en Cuba,* 182.
3. Cubans call monetary incentives material incentives.
4. While many authors question the validity of official Cuban economic

statistics from the 1980s, independent analyses by Zimbalist, Mesa-Lago, and others support the trend if not the magnitude of growth given by the official statistics. The Banco Nacional de Cuba reports that Gross Social Product grew an average 7.3 percent from 1981 to 1985. Criticism of these figures has focused on the wholesale price reform (increases in prices) for which supposedly the growth figures have not been adjusted. Nevertheless, Mesa-Lago does admit that Cuba attained "healthy growth rates" in the early 1980s, before the economy suffered a significant decline in 1986. For a full discussion on Cuba's economic performance of the 1980s, *see* Mesa-Lago, "The Cuban Economy of the 1980s" in Horowitz, ed., *Cuban Communism*. Zimbalist, ed., *Cuba's Socialist Economy*.

5. Carranza, Gutierrez, y Monreal, *Cuba: La Restructuración de la Economía*, 2.
6. In Spanish: Sistema de Dirección y Planificación de la Economía.
7. Pérez-Lopez, *Cuba's Second Economy*, 224.
8. Mesa-Lago, "Cuban Economy of the 1980s" in José Luis Rodríguez, *Estrategia del Desarrollo Económico en Cuba*.
9. Theriot, "Cuba Faces the Economic Realities."
10. Reuters, June 6, 1986.
11. According to José Luis Rodríguez, Cuba's finance minister, it was 8.8 percent. Mesa-Lago, "Cuban Economy of the 1980s," estimates eighty-four percent and Andrés Oppenheimer, eighty-seven percent.
12. Oppenheimer, *Castro's Final Hour.*

4

THE EARLY '90S: A VERY "SPECIAL PERIOD"

We have been left outside the world's two economic
structures. We are hanging in the air, trying to find a
new place to insert ourselves.

Ernesto Meléndez
President of the Cuban Cooperation Committee[1]

Cubans watched the dismemberment of the Soviet Union with the same
stupefaction as the rest of the world, but for them it had profound
implications on their everyday lives. Without oil from the Soviet Union,
public transportation was a disaster; a three-hour wait for the bus was
common. Constant blackouts interrupted life at home and at work. In
fact, Cubans used to say that in those days they did not suffer blackouts or *apagones*, but *alumbrones* or illuminations, since the lights
went off and rarely came back on. The supply of running water was
erratic at best, forcing many schools to close down and hospitals to
operate under extreme conditions. There were no spare parts for consumer goods, no fertilizers, and no food. On the roads, bicycles
substituted for cars[2] while oxen replaced tractors on the fields.[3] Soon,
Cubans began to refer to this situation as *el periodo especial,* and a
very "special period" it was, indeed. Havana looked like a war-torn
city, full of fears, needs, and frustrations. The government called it a
"special period in time of peace."

Factories closed down. With no jobs to go to, people stayed at home
while getting paid sixty percent of their salaries. That was the
government's answer to unemployment. But people soon found that
even with their meager salaries, they always had more money in their
pockets than they could spend. There were simply not enough things to
buy. Many people developed varicose veins as they stood in endless
lines waiting for scarce rationing-card goods. Prices were kept low in
the official market but scarcity was rampant; people were hungry and
desperate. In the black market, prices were skyrocketing. The term

SEAN SPRAGUE

"Do it for Cuba," reads the sign. But do what?

"special period" became a euphemism for what was really an almost impossible situation. It was a harsh reality to confront and a matter of life and death for many. The world was waiting for Castro to fall while Castro waited for the perestroika-glasnost nightmare to end. There was no time for an ideological debate, only pragmatic solutions.

Living in the "Special Period"

Eddie had a hard job: he worked for a government he didn't understand anymore. In his small office it was 100 degrees, the humidity was oppressive, and with no electricity he had only the dim sunlight from the window to write his report. He was a bureaucrat "in the good sense of the word, not like those who used power for their own benefit." He was supposed to set an example. He was also supposed to know better, to have more confidence in the future, to understand the government's strategy . . . but he didn't. And that was the hardest part of his job: not understanding. He was hungry; back home there had been only enough breakfast to feed his two daughters, so he and his wife had gone to work on an empty stomach. After a ten-mile bicycle ride to the office, he was starving. What was going to happen to Cuba? He worked for the government, but he couldn't answer this question any better than anyone else. According to Fidel and his cohorts, the situation would improve when Gorbachev's experiment was over. The good news was that rumors of a military coup in Russia were becoming more and more frequent. Maybe Fidel was right. We just have to make do until the *real* socialists take over the Russian government again.

While wishing the worst for Gorbachev and his followers, Martica's voice interrupted his thoughts. "Eddie! It's time to go, the sunlight is almost gone!" She was right, he had to leave soon and pick up some food on the way home. He searched his pockets and found 100 pesos, one third of his salary. Last time he went food shopping he couldn't find much; maybe he'd have better luck today. He left his papers and joined Martica at the front door. She had an empty bag in her hands and was going to get food at the black market: chicken and rice.

"Great!" he said, "let's go together. I have a couple of good contacts."

Martica looked at him skeptically. "You? With good black market contacts?"

No wonder prices kept going up, she thought. Even loyal party members like Eddie were getting their food in the black market. It was the special period, and everyone had to rely on the black market. After all, there was no red market anymore. The Russians were gone, and with them the so-called red markets where Soviets had offered products purchased in special dollar stores in exchange for rum or cigars. From Eddie's face, she could tell the situation was much worse than she had thought. He had been looking at the numbers this afternoon and inflation in the black market was staggering. Still, he tried to disguise his concern. "Don't worry. It won't be long before things get better and prices in the black market fall."

"I'm not worried," quipped Martica, "I pay in dollars."

"Are you out of your mind?" blurted Eddie. "Do you know what will happen if they catch you with dollars? I hope you're not carrying them now!"

After hopping on her bike, she proudly showed him a green roll with three 10-dollar bills. Martica had family in Miami; she received her dollars regularly. That was how she made ends meet and she was willing to risk jail for it. She had made up her mind. "I'm going to have chicken and rice with my family tonight and that's it." She offered him one of the bills, but he pulled back defensively. She insisted, wiggling the bill in front of him, "Come on, you can't buy anything decent with your 100 pesos! That's not even worth a dollar."

Eddie shook his head and left as fast as his legs and bike could carry him. He had seen it too many times—people disappearing after going out to buy things with dollars. Holding dollars in Cuba was illegal.

TABLE **4.1**   The Two Faces of the Cuban Peso:
Cuban Pesos Per US Dollar

	1990	1991	1992	1993
Official	1.00	1.00	1.00	1.00
Black Market	7.00	20.00	45.00	100.00*

*At one point in 1993 the exchange rate reached 160 pesos per U.S. dollar.
Source: Banco Nacional de Cuba, 1996 Report.

TABLE **4.2**   Too Many Pesos Chasing Too Few Goods

	1989	1990	1991	1992	1993
Pesos in Circulation	4,163	4,986	6,663	8,361	11,043
Percentage of GDP	20	24	39	51	67

Source: CEPAL, *La Economia Cubana.* Fondo de Cultura Economica, 1997.

There were hundreds of people in prison for having committed that crime. The reason? Most dollars came from relatives in Miami and it was unfair for those who didn't have family in exile. At least that's what *they* said. Whatever the logic, whatever the concept of fair and unfair, he wasn't gambling, no matter how bad the situation got.

Still, he couldn't help thinking that Martica was right. He couldn't buy much with 100 pesos. He had been studying the figures this afternoon. The official exchange rate had been kept at the ridiculous rate of one Cuban peso per US dollar while the informal (black) market rate had jumped to more than 100 pesos per dollar.

Since demand kept growing—the government kept paying salaries, social security and subsidies—in the face of a continuous decline in production and supply, the number of pesos in circulation kept increasing. In turn, excess pesos in circulation propelled the price of the dollar in the black market as well as the prices of goods. Supply problems in the formal state trading system generated rapid growth in the informal market; by 1993, the informal market had grown to seven times its 1989 size.

He knew that in spite of price controls in the formal market, inflation was soaring in the black market. With his salary he couldn't feed his family anymore. He bought some pasta and cooking oil for dinner, although he would have preferred butter. But only the *pinchos* (a slang word for members of the military) were eating butter these days. The agreement with East Germany—Cuba's long-time supplier of powdered milk—had been suspended. No milk, no butter. He couldn't afford the meat or eggs either. Pasta and cooking oil would have to do for tonight; tomorrow would be another day. His wife had been trying to convince him that she should get a job in a hotel and earn some dollars. Tonight she confronted him: either a job in a hotel or Miami—it was his choice.

That evening after dinner, Eddie took his two-year-old daughter for a walk through the dark streets of their neighborhood. The street had been in total darkness for a long time. Up ahead he saw something different. His daughter noticed it too. A streetlight was on. There had been no light on those streets for almost three years—three "very special" years. His two-year-old daughter, who had known nothing else but life in the "special period," didn't even know what a streetlight was.

"Daddy, I didn't know there were lights on the streets, I had never seen one" said the little girl with wonderment.

Smiling, Eddie looked at his daughter, "Well, maybe it's a wishing star, honey."

The Cuban Government: Keeping Cool When the Heat Is On

The honeymoon was over. When Soviet President Mikhail Gorbachev visited Cuba in April, 1989, he made clear that the long-standing sponsorship of the island was coming to an end. Future trade would be conducted in convertible currency and subsidies would be cut. Other CMEA[4] countries were adopting an equally tough stance toward Cuba. As imports fell dramatically, Castro railed against what he viewed as the disloyalty of the Soviet Union and the CMEA members. The suddenness of the Soviet decision left Cuba in the lurch, unprepared for the loss of its socialist trading partners. In Moscow, the press and the congress had begun to question Soviet aid to Cuba. Criticism of Castro's iron hand and political repression were widespread. Glasnost unleashed the suppressed criticism Russians had for their forty years of paternalism with Cuba.

In 1989, the Cuban regime was also rocked by the trial and execution of General Arnaldo Ochoa Sanchez, a top military official who was convicted for a drug smuggling conspiracy. Many saw this affair as a crack in the Cuban system that could potentially lead to the unraveling of the communist state, a process that was well underway in Central and Eastern Europe. However, Fidel used the scandal to purge the government of dozens of reform-minded officials, including the powerful interior minister, General José Abrantes.[5]

The Cuban government attributed the collapse of socialism in Eastern Europe to a failure of leadership, not a failure of the system. Socialism was in Cuba to stay. Using the mass media, the government spread the message that European leadership had committed a serious mistake in making concessions to the enemies of socialism.[6] Stories of dismal conditions in the new democracies were circulated as proof of the foolishness of abandoning socialism. Journalists in the Soviet Union fired back with bitter criticism of Castro's regime. News of a growing opposition movement and calls to support a referendum in Cuba were part of the Soviet attack on the Cuban government.

News from the outside world also became a scarce commodity for Cuban citizens. *Sputnik* and *Moscow News,* two widely read Soviet Spanish-language magazines, were banned by the government when they began criticizing the regime in 1989. By 1991, all Soviet magazines and newspapers had been removed from newsstands and a key source of information for Cubans had disappeared. The government was in control.

The 1989 Crisis: An Economy in Free Fall

From 1989 to 1993, the Cuban economy responded to the communist debacle in the Soviet Union by going into free fall. Gross domestic product (GDP) fell more than forty percent during the period: –2.9 percent in 1990, –10.7 percent in 1991, –11.6 percent in 1992 and –14.9 percent in 1993.

FIGURE 4.1   GDP Plunge 1989–93

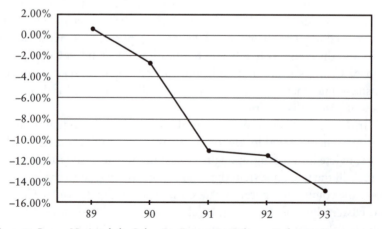

Sources: Banco Nacional de Cuba. La Economia Cubana: Reformas Estructurales y desempeño en los Noventa, CEPAL.

TABLE 4.3   Without Fertilizers and Tractors Sugar Production Was Cut in Half

	1989	1990	1991	1992	1993
Sugar Production	8	8.4	7.6	6.3	4.2

Source: Banco Nacional de Cuba, 1995.

TABLE 4.4   Exports and Imports Plummet

	1989	1990	1991	1992	1993
Exports	5,993	5,940	3,563	2,522	1,992
Imports	10,171	9,271	5,291	2,894	2,363
Trade Balance	−4,178	−3,331	−1,728	−372	−371
Official Transfers*	3,000	1,000	500	50	50
Current Account Balance	−1,164	−2,289	−1,140	−140	−319

Sources: La Economía Cubana: Reformas Estructurales y Desempeño de los Noventa, Anexo Estadístico, CEPAL, Agosto, 1997; and *Evolución Económica Durante 1994,* 1996, Cepal.

The cut-off of Soviet aid and the collapse of commercial arrangements with the socialist bloc—which had accounted for over eighty percent of Cuba's trade—were nothing less than devastating for the economy of the island.

With the changes in its external trade relations, exports plunged from $5.9 billion in 1989 to $1.9 billion in 1993, due mainly to the collapse in sugar production from eight million tons in 1989 to 4.2 million tons in 1993. This shock was partly the result of the USSR elimination of its preferential price policy for sugar and nickel. Total subsidies to Cuba averaged US$2,100 million per year during the 1960–90 period. The collapse in sugar production also reflected the lack of access to imported inputs and the break-up of large, capital-intensive state farms into smaller labor-intensive cooperatives. Also in 1992 the U.S. embargo was tightened with the Cuban Democracy Act, or the Torricelli Act in recognition of its principal sponsor, Congressman Robert Torricelli. The principal provisions of the act were to prohibit subsidiaries of U.S. companies from trading with Cuba, which had been legal since 1975, and to restrict ships that traded with Cuba from docking in U.S. ports. The Torricelli act became an important additional blow to

This little girl is the only one who has it easy when it's time to go to work.

Cuba's possibilities for economic recuperation.

Imports were brought down from $8.1 billion in 1989 to $2.3 billion in 1993 in order to contain the trade deficit, in line with the meager external financing. By 1992, Soviet aid had been cut from $3 billion in 1989 to only $50 million.

Too Little, Too Late

Driven more by external reality than internal conviction, Cuban policymakers began to introduce a few market reforms in 1990. Without the massive Soviet aid on which Cuba had become so dependent, the government had little choice but to introduce the changes of the "special period." This was not a widespread economic reform. Rather, it was a set of measures designed to achieve the following limited objectives: save energy, increase food production, expand markets for exports and imports, and attract foreign investment as a key source of hard currency, technology, and markets. In order to make these changes and legalize private investment, Cuba's National Assembly passed in 1992 a number of amendments to the 1976 constitution providing the legal basis for transferring state property to joint ventures with foreign partners. They also abolished the state monopoly on foreign trade.

The changes introduced during the "special period" were concentrated in the external sector: foreign investment, international trade, and tourism. The basic strategy was to insert Cuba into international markets without making any dramatic changes in the internal socioeconomic structure. The government wanted an isolated enclave of foreign investment and tourism, which could provide the hard currency and resources needed to maintain the rest of the social structure unchanged. In other words, the idea was to substitute Soviet aid with foreign investment and tourism and hope for the best—and the best in the eyes of the Cuban government would be to wake up from the nightmare that Gorbachev had instigated with his *glasnost* and *perestroika*. Was that possible? Many in the Cuban government thought Gorbachev's days were numbered.

In the meantime, the government implemented a series of austerity measures to cope with the shortage in foreign exchange, the decline in production, and the collapse in imports. The austerity program included:[7]

- Reducing fuel deliveries to both the state and private sectors by up to eighty percent
- Substituting cars and buses with bicycles
- Substituting tractors with oxen and mules
- Shutting down the nickel-processing plant and oil refinery to save energy (there was not enough crude oil to process anyway)
- Reinstating rationing for food and clothing
- Returning to labor-intensive programs in agriculture and displacing workers from the cities to the countryside. Thousands of people were ordered to leave their workplaces in the cities to join the brigades of *movilizados* and move to the countryside to perform labor-intensive agricultural jobs.

Foreign Investment: A Joint Venture with Capitalism

Perhaps the most important change during this period was the 1992 constitutional reform allowing ownership by mixed enterprises and the transfer of state ownership to joint ventures with foreign capital. For the first time since the revolution, an amendment to the Constitution set limits to socialist ownership. Article 14 of the Constitution now reads: "In the Republic of Cuba rules the socialist system of economy based on the people's socialist ownership of the *fundamental*[8] means of production."[9]

By using the word fundamental, which was absent from the earlier version, the new Constitution opened the legal possibility of private ownership. Article 15 of the Constitution was also changed to empower the Council of Ministers to transfer goods from the socialist sector to any natural or juridical entity that would serve the social and economic development of the country. This important adjustment effectively expanded Law-Decree 50 of 1982 and allowed the formation of joint ventures. Under the basic provisions of the new law, foreign partners were allowed:

1. Up to forty-nine percent ownership
2. Total exemption on taxes
3. Unrestricted repatriation of profits in hard currency
4. Freedom to hire foreign executives

With these changes in the foreign investment law, the number of joint ventures jumped from two in 1990 to 112 in 1993.[10]

Devaluation? No! Foreign Exchange Rationing? Yes!

Faced with the collapse in export revenues, the Cuban government enacted a set of measures designed to mitigate the social impact of the adjustment. These measures generated important economic disequilibria, which in turn provoked additional reforms.

The decision to ration foreign exchange rather than devalue the currency has generated serious inefficiencies. In market economies, an adjustment to an external shock of this magnitude would have required a massive devaluation to reduce the demand for imports and increase the profitability of export and import-competing sectors, so as to efficiently return to external balance. Unfortunately, there is a political price to pay with this policy. Such real devaluations require a lower real wage, an unpopular decision opposed by the National Assembly and the government. The finance minister made this position clear: "Taking into account the positive experiences of other countries like China and Vietnam, we avoided a sudden currency devaluation. This would have added terrible (social) consequences to the already difficult economic crisis faced by the country."[11]

Thus, given a centrally planned economy, Cuban officials reacted to the sudden shortage of foreign exchange not by devaluing, but by rationing foreign exchange and administratively distributing dollars to different sectors. This was supposed to ensure "the equitable distribution of the limited supply of resources available to all social groups—prices would not rise in response to the fall in supply, but the limited supply of products and services would be shared equitably among the population as a whole at subsidized prices."[12]

In spite of the objectives of the Cuban government, substituting this arbitrary process for devaluation generated serious inefficiencies for which Cuba has been paying dearly. Since products are neither more expensive nor more profitable—as would have happened with devaluation—shortages develop as output contracts and demand grows in response to low, controlled prices. In other words, the system does not generate the price incentives to produce or save dollars. Imports are extremely cheap at the distorted official exchange rate of one peso per US$1, so there is an unrealistic incentive to import. Dollars were assigned proportionally to "strategic" sectors without regard to efficiency.

Moreover, the efforts to attract foreign private capital in the tourist sector increased the circulation of dollars in the economy and the proliferation of a black market for goods. The original intention of opening tourism alone to foreign investment was soon defeated by realities. When important export sectors like nickel, tobacco, citrus and biotechnology lagged behind due to obsolete technology and lack of hard currency to buy inputs, the government opened up these sectors to foreign investment. Only sugar, the traditional source of foreign exchange in Cuba, remained closed to direct foreign investment. Nevertheless, it continued to perform poorly; in the 1994–95 harvest, sugar production plunged to 3.3 million tons, the worst performance in the country's history. Eventually, Cubans had to abandon their misconceived notions of nationalism and accept private investment in sugar.

The Price of Spending

Given the government reluctance to devalue, Cubans were left with more purchasing power—measured at official prices—than the actual supply of goods available. This led to greater rationing and higher black market prices for goods. Also, insufficient adjustment led to a fiscal deficit that mounted to 30.4 percent of GDP in 1993.

The government could not stop spending even though exports, the economy, and fiscal revenues were collapsing. Given the absence of external financing and of internal capital markets, the government had very little choice but to cover the deficit by printing money. The result: the economy was flooded with liquidity. The number of pesos in circulation increased from five billion in 1990 to 11.4 billion in 1994.

In a market economy, excess liquidity creates inflation. In a centrally

TABLE 4.5   A Growing Fiscal Deficit

	1989	1990	1991	1992	1993
Fiscal Deficit As %GDP	–6.7	–9.4	–21.4	–29.7	–30.4

Source: *Evolución Económica Durante 1994, 1996*, CEPAL.

planned economy, the effects are different. Since official prices do not change and people have more money to spend than products to buy, huge shortages and black markets develop. By the end of 1993, the official exchange rate was one peso per U.S. dollar, while it reached 130 pesos per dollar in the black market.

The situation worsened every day: high inflation in the growing informal market, widening fiscal deficits, scarcity in the formal sector, the plunge of the Cuban peso, and the creation of a parallel economy were creating an unsustainable situation. Carranza, Gutiérrez and Monreal, three prominent Cuban economists, summarized the situation:

> The level of wages received by the population had been in excess of that necessary to obtain the basic level of rationed goods, but insufficient to cover price inflation within the informal market. This created pressure on part of the population to enter informal markets not only as buyers but as sellers, since this was the only way in which they could obtain the income necessary to continue to purchase in those markets. This generated an upward spiral of speculation. It also intensified the separation of a growing part of the labor force and tended to convert into a permanent rupture what had been a temporary separation.
>
> All this had a very negative impact on a worker's society, not only in economic terms but also in ideological terms given that the wage—the economic and social reason to work—ceased to be the fundamental route for obtaining individual and family well being.[13]

Setting the Limits of Change

Although the government voiced its decision to make the "changes required" to face the crisis, Cuban intellectuals and policymakers maintained the socialist orientation of the system.

In summary, the reforms would permit the transition from a classical model of socialism to another kind of socialism which would require giving the market an active role, neither exclusive nor dominant in the allocation of resources and in the economy as a whole.[13]

In a speech at the National Assembly, Fidel emphasized this point:

We will have to improve and perfect socialism, make it efficient but not destroy it. The illusion that capitalism is going to solve our problems is an absurd and crazy chimera for which the masses will pay dearly. This is another reason why, not only because socialism is more just, more honorable, and more human in every sense, but because it is the only system that would provide us with the resources to keep our social conquests.[14]

Cuba is a socialist regime. This is important to understand when viewing the particular speed and sequencing of the reforms the government has undertaken and the great caution with which they have been introduced. Cuban officials considered the reforms in the former Soviet Union a tragic disappointment while Latin American reforms have been dismissed as socially unjust: "The neo-liberal model adopted in Latin America characterized by price liberalization, the reduction of real wages and welfare programs was never consulted with the people and increased dramatically the already terrifying levels of inequality in those countries."[15]

As dramatic as the adjustments may have seemed, the government's actions proved to be too little, too late and generated further imbalances that, in turn, led to more reforms. By 1993, the government realized that the solution to the crisis was not to be found in cosmetic changes made at the periphery of the system or in the hope of returning to the arms of the Russians. The strategy would require profound revisions of the socialist order and of its incentive structure. Subsequent reforms have included legalizing hard currency, creating agricultural cooperatives, introducing monetary incentives to increase labor productivity, opening free markets for farmers and artisans, legalizing the establishment of foreign firms with one hundred percent foreign capital, authorizing free zones, and allowing 157 economic activities to be performed by self-employed workers. These are some of the real changes the Cuban government has made since 1993 when it realized that reform could not be confined to the external sector. What impact have these reforms had on Cuban society? How have they affected the social and political equilibrium? Clearly, for some they are threats to stability and the established order.[16] For others, they are like streetlights in a Havana neighborhood that has long gone dark.

Notes

1. Oppenheimer, *Castro's Final Hour.*
2. 200,000 were imported from China. In 1992, there were an estimated 500,000 bicycles in Havana. *See* Julio Carranza, "Cuba: Los Retos de la Economia."
3. By 1991, the government had ordered the domestication of 300,000 oxen to replace 30,000 Soviet tractors.
4. Council of Mutual Economic Assistance (CMEA). The economic trading unit comprised of the Eastern European countries and the U.S.S.R.
5. Oppenheimer, *Castro's Final Hour.*
6. Domínguez, "The Political Impact of Cuba."
7. See Pérez-Lopez, *Cuba's Second Economy.*
8. Emphasis by the author.
9. Constitution of the Republic of Cuba, 1992.
10. CEPAL. La Inversión Extranjera en Cuba Aspectos Recientes. LC/MEX/L.286, November 22, 1995. *Also see* Omar Pérez, "El Comercio Exterior."
11. José Luis Rodríguez, finance minister, at the World Economic Forum in Davos, February, 1996.
12. Carranza, Gutiérrez and Monreal, *Cuba: Restructuring the Economy,* 14.
13. Carranza, Gutiérrez and Monreal, *Cuba: Restructuring the Economy,* 15.
14. Carranza, Gutiérrez y Monreal, *Cuba: La Restructuración de la Economía.*
15. Fidel Castro, Speech at the National Assembly, December 28, 1993.
16. Oswaldo Martínez, Representative from Sagua de Tánamo to the National Assembly, National Assembly Debates, Granma, December 29, 1993.

5

HUNTING FOR DOLLARS

> We are doomed to choose, and every choice may entail
> an irreparable loss.
>
> Isaiah Berlin[1]

By July 1993, Cuba was on the verge of collapse. Political and economic survival demanded drastic changes, but how far could the government go without giving up socialism all together? Not surprisingly, many government officials were afraid of the answer. Ideology was in the balance; so was survival.

Life for most Cubans had become unbearable. People were starving, salaries were worth nothing, and inflation in the black market was soaring. The only thing that made a difference was dollars. Those with families in exile or with access to tourist dollars could survive. Dollar holdings were still illegal, but since 1989, Cubans had learned that many laws simply didn't make sense. Illegality became a way of life for many.

For the government, the situation had become totally unmanageable. The fiscal deficit had ballooned to unsustainable levels: over thirty percent of GDP, or five billion pesos in 1993.[2] In spite of the widening fiscal gap, the government kept spending. Salaries and social programs—the core of the socialist promise—remained unchanged. Liquidity grew from twenty percent of GDP in 1989 to 66.5 percent of GDP in 1993. While GDP contracted, the deficit expanded. Consequently, from 1989 to 1993 the fiscal deficit as a percentage of GDP had grown almost ninety percent. At the same time, seventy percent of state enterprises were operating at a loss, most of them with insufficient supplies. Although they were excessively subsidized and highly inefficient, state enterprises were kept open to avoid greater unemployment.

The dollar—officially pegged at one peso per U.S. dollar—shot through the roof at 170 pesos per dollar in the black market. It was illegal to trade in the black market but no one seemed to care. After all, the average monthly salary was 120 pesos—barely enough to buy a pound of pork. The black market had become the most important source of food for Cubans, and prices in that market were skyrocketing. Dollar remittances from families in exile began to increase as they tried to help hungry relatives on the island. The precipice looked dangerously near.

Big Daddy Goes Broke

The problem was clear: the country was producing much less, while workers were being paid the same. The government had promised there would be no salary adjustments, no unemployment and no devaluation. But the Cuban government—Big Daddy—couldn't protect the populace indefinitely. There were too many pesos chasing too few goods.

Usually, governments go broke when they consistently spend more than what they earn. Under these circumstances, they must either explicitly or implicitly default on their commitments. Explicit default usually takes the form of outright repudiation of debts and other obligations such as free university education or social security. When political considerations preclude explicit default, implicit default takes the form of accelerated inflation, which erodes the value of people's salaries and holdings. This is what happened in Cuba. The government was broke, but refused to acknowledge it explicitly. Instead, it had subjected the country to the consequences of implicit default: galloping inflation and salary erosion.

In a socialist economy like Cuba's, the macroeconomic effects of the government going bankrupt are very straightforward. The public sector is all there is; there is no private sector to counterbalance or complicate the story. By 1993, the government was in default and it was taking the *implicit* form of money overhang: longer lines for food and rampant inflation in the black market. Making this default explicit would necessarily include outright fiscal and real adjustments. Although there were many choices, all were very unpopular: cuts in the *libreta* (rationing card), reductions in subsidies to inefficient state enterprises, layoffs, price increases on housing and utilities, and paring down social programs, among others.

In the external sector, the lack of fiscal resources meant the government simply didn't have enough dollars to import food. Prior to the crisis, much of the food provided through the *libreta* was imported. By 1989, a full fifty-one percent of the calories consumed in Cuba came from abroad. The food program of the special period, designed to achieve self-sufficiency, had been unsuccessful. The limited array of products offered in the *libreta* were only providing nine hundred calories a day, less than half an adult's caloric requirements. Nutritional and vitamin deficiencies had caused blindness and paralysis in over 45,000 Cubans. The limited reforms of the 1990–93 period, designed to shield the population from harm, had instead subjected them to severe suffering. The end of the system seemed near. It was around this time that writer and reporter Andrés Oppenheimer published his book, Castro's Final Hour, which was publicized as the "eyewitness account of the disintegration of Castro's Cuba." Once again, everyone predicted the fall of the system.

As Cuba sank into the worst crisis of its history, more and more Cubans were anxious to bail ship. Despite the revolutionary rhetoric from the leadership, the sense of failure was widespread and the values of the revolution were rapidly waning. The government could no longer provide the public services that had been the pride of the revolution. The government was broke, and the hopes of an egalitarian society were shattered. Much like in the early '60s, Cubans were fleeing the island. The new exodus though, was inspired not by fear of the revolution but by disenchantment and desperation. The time was ripe for long needed reforms. Cuba's economic and political survival depended on them.

What Went Wrong?

The strategy implemented in 1990 failed. Promotion of foreign investment and tourism brought in more dollars, but not enough. Besides, the strategy suffered from some fundamental flaws.

Cuba had long been a subsidized economy. The Soviet bloc had provided hard currency in the form of direct and indirect subsidies to finance import levels of about US$8 billion, or almost US$800 per inhabitant—an extremely high figure considering that Venezuela, whose population is more than double Cuba's, registered a similar level of imports in the same year. By 1993, the economy had to adjust to less than US$2 billion—less than a third.

In essence, the Cuban government for years had received a net income transfer from the Soviet bloc. Those resources came free of cost into government accounts. The government, in turn, used the money at its discretion for various social or military needs. In 1989 alone, unilateral transfers from the Soviet bloc to the Cuban government totaled US$3 billion.

Indirect subsidies supplemented these direct subsidies. The CMEA used to pay Cuba well above the international price for sugar. The average price of Cuban sugar exports in 1989 was US$438 per ton, while in

TABLE 5.1   Without Russian Aid the Cuban Socialist State Crumbled

	1989	1993
Total exports	5,993	1,992
Total imports	8,608	2,373
Trade deficit	2,615	−383
Soviet Aid*	3,000	50

Source: The ECLAC Report, 1995.
* Called Unilateral Official Transfers in the ECLAC Report, 1995.

TABLE 5.2   Sugar Prices Turned Sour

	1989	1995
Sugar exports US$ (000)	3,120,000	704,000
Sugar exports in Tons	7,119,000	2,600,000
Average price per ton US$	438.26	270.76
'89 Exports at '95 prices	1,927,606	
Difference with '89 exports	1,192,394	

Sources: ECLAC, *La Economía Cubana en 1996: Resultados, Problemas y Perspectivas.* Centro de Estudios de la Economía Cubana (CEEC), Universidad de la Habana, January 1997.

1995 it was US$270. Swings in international prices aside, sugar exports provided a hefty indirect subsidy to the Cuban government. As shown above, in 1989 the sugar subsidy was around US$1.2 billion.

With these direct and indirect subsidies, the government could finance a high level of imports and a generous *libreta.* Soviet aid constituted far more than just an inflow of dollars; it was the source of discretionary spending in the hands of the state.

Foreign Investment for Foreign Aid?

It should have been clear that the idea of substituting transfers and aid with tourism and foreign direct investment made no logical sense. Dollars that came into the country as foreign direct investment would simply have to go back out to pay for the machinery and equipment of new projects. And the dollars that tourism brought in would have to go out to pay for the imported goods consumed by the tourists. Foreign investment dollars, in contrast to Soviet aid, *were not* going to provide the state with discretionary income to support the *libreta,* social services, or the military. The strategy of reforming as little as possible and leaving the system as is—except for a few minor changes—in order to spare Cubans from an "inhumane economic adjustment" was not only unfeasible, it simply didn't happen. Cubans became significantly poorer in spite of the absence of adjustment measures.

While Cubans maintained the right to buy goods and the money to pay for them, there were simply no goods available. Salaries remained unchanged while the government's supply of goods dwindled, which meant that people were left with an excess of money. What did they do with it? They tried to spend it in the black market, pushing prices and the unofficial dollar rate through the roof. To top it off, the government continued to prohibit residents from holding dollars, making the scarcity of foreign exchange even more acute.

The state was losing control. The growing black market for dollars and goods was completely out of the state's reach. The size of these markets provided incentives for everyone working for the state to smuggle goods into the black market. As the situation worsened, remittances increased, giving greater economic power to households and the black market.

While the state-run socialist economy crumbled, a private informal economy was flourishing. Dollars in the hands of the government were decreasing, but the average citizen had more dollars than ever before. Foreign investors, tourists, and families abroad fueled the informal black market with dollars while the government desperately hunted for them abroad.

Given the absurdity of this situation, the government had no choice but to introduce some changes. Its motivation was twofold: to turn the situation around for the benefit of all and, to regain control.

As the government explored the possibilities, it became painfully clear that some policies may be good for the long term, but were incapable of resolving short-term disequilibria. Over the long run, foreign investment would help Cuba produce more and export more; but demand would far exceed supply for a long time. Cubans were attempting to spend more than what they produced. There were two solutions to this situation:

1. Usually, *demand side* policies—those that reduce demand to meet supply levels—are more effective in the short term. For example, a devaluation and/or fiscal cutback would immediately reduce the purchasing power of consumers and put supply and demand in equilibrium. However, the leadership in Cuba

Cubans get a taste of fast food thanks to foreign investment.

    opposed devaluation and the resulting depreciation of real
    salaries.

2.   A more attractive strategy in the short run was to substitute the
       Soviet rent with exile remittances and tourist dollars.

    Little is known about how the government finally changed the economic strategy. Nevertheless, all indications are that the decision was made to substitute the Russian rent with dollars sent home by Cuban exiles to their families and by dollars brought in by tourists. To complement the strategy, they implemented a fiscal adjustment by reducing government expenditures and raising taxes to increase income. As unpopular as many of these measures were, the government did keep one promise: the Cuban peso was not officially devalued.

The Government: Still Empty-handed

    From the government's perspective, this economic strategy still suffered from a severe shortcoming. While the Russian rent passed directly into government hands, remittances and tourist money went directly to the private sector. There was another problem. Cubans in the private sector who received dollars were anxious to spend them on products and services *inside* Cuba. But dollars could only buy them products and services abroad. Consequently, the government needed to establish a mechanism by which people could use those dollars to buy products and services locally so the government could get its hands on them. The idea was not only to sell products and services so Cubans could use the highly priced foreign currency, but for the government to get control over it. The bottom line of the strategy was to introduce a new type of "export," this time directed not to the Russians or members of the CMEA but to the Cubans who had dollars in Cuba: those who received remittances from Miami and who earned dollars from the tourist trade.

The reforms designed to achieve this objective were quickly implemented between the second half of 1993 and 1994:

1. The first and most obvious change was the *legalization of dollar holdings* so Cubans could freely transact with them and attract remittances from families abroad.

2. Second, *government-owned retail stores in dollars were opened* so Cubans could buy goods in hard currency. In this way, the government could get its hands on part of the private dollar holdings. Prices in dollars would be high in order to get high margins to finance the fiscal deficit. By 1997 the government-owned retail sector was booming together with the service sector in dollars. Internal hard currency sales in dollars rose 17.8 percent in 1997 reaching 740 million dollars for the January–December period.

3. Third, to increase the supply of goods the government proceeded with the *cooperativization of agriculture and the re-opening of the free farmer's markets*. These reforms in agriculture aimed to increase local food production. By changing the big state-owned farms into cooperatives, they also wanted to change the incentive mechanisms for workers. Now, cooperative members were responsible for their production and could share in the profits. On the other hand, the reopening of the free farmers' markets—closed since 1986—allowed farmers to again sell to the public part of their production at free prices, but this time, in dollars.

4. Fourth, to increase efficiency and local production, the government began a process of *decentralization of state owned enterprises and joint ventures* with foreign enterprises. By converting state-owned enterprises into profit centers, the government could eliminate subsidies, reduce the fiscal deficit, increase exports, and sell more products to Cubans in dollars and in pesos.

5. Cubans not only wanted more goods, they wanted more ser-
    vices, which the government was unable to provide in those
    days. The legalization of *self-employment* and the liberaliza-
    tion of over 150 services was meant to address this problem.
    The services included hairdressers, plumbers, mechanics, and
    the well-known paladares, or small family-owned restaurants.
    University professions were excluded. Cubans could now pay
    for these services formerly provided only by state companies.
    How would the government get a share of the money spent on
    these private services? The answer was simple: taxes.

6. The fiscal deficit had to be cut and tax reform was a must. The
    government enacted a series of measures designed to increase
    fiscal income and reduce expenditures. For the first time in
    thirty-five years, the government decided to implement a tax
    reform aimed principally at the small emerging private sector,
    especially the self-employed. The government was smart enough
    not to tax dollar remittances. Although some leaders proposed
    taxing peso salaries, the measure was extremely unpopular and
    was defeated in the National Assembly.

These reforms gave the government, and Cubans, room to breathe.
For example, a family that received US$100 from relatives in Miami
was no longer forced to spend them in the black market. They could
now legally shop in dollars in a variety of places. They could, for example, spend forty dollars in the farmer's market, ten dollars in the
paladares, twenty dollars in the state-run retail stores, where they could
also buy goods produced by the joint ventures, and thirty dollars on
services provided by the self-employed. The economy had become less
socialist and the government was back in control.

The Two Cubas: Living in the '90s

Jorge tossed a bottle of spoiled milk in the trash with disgust. The
refrigerator was broken, his ten-year-old son's breakfast was ruined,
and he was late. He began to make some phone calls. To the hospital:
he'd be late this Saturday morning, could someone else see his patients?
To a friend: did he know anyone who could fix this useless Russian
relic? To another friend: did he know where to find spare parts for his
Atlant Soviet refrigerator? Cuba hadn't bought a single refrigerator from
its sole Russian supplier for the past five years. Spare parts hadn't come
in since then either. There had to be a black market for them, he was

sure; he had the morning to find out.

Blanquita, his neighbor, was just arriving from a rough night *jineteando*.[3] Her 300-peso salary as a psychologist couldn't pay for her nice clothes, or for the clothing and food she wanted for her son either. That's why she had followed the example of many university graduates in the '90s and was moonlighting as a *jinetera* or prostitute. Since university professions were not included among those liberated for self-employment, university graduates could only moonlight in activities allowed for self-employment. Many did it in legalized services as plumbers, hairdressers, or taxi drivers. Others preferred *jineterismo*.

She could easily make US$100 in one night. She just had to go out dancing, eat in a nice restaurant, and have a little sex. "Isn't that what free women do everywhere," she thought?

Jorge's face turned into a sad smile when he saw Blanquita with the same tight yellow dress from the night before and with her tired green eyes. "I think you're beginning to like this, Blanquita. It's one thing to go out and earn some dollars for your children moonlighting as a prostitute, but to enjoy it? That's something else. You should be ashamed of yourself."

"Listen, Jorge," she fired back, "I never said I didn't enjoy it. Besides, I wouldn't do it if I didn't like it—get that into your stubborn revolutionary head." She didn't like being called a prostitute. She just wanted to go out, talk to people from other countries, and get a taste of what a "normal" life could be—like the people you see in the movies. Yes, she was a "struggler," or *luchadora*. That's why she began to *jinetear*—for the money. But now she did it because it was the only way to get out of her miserable, boring life here. "I want to live and have some fun. I am sick and tired of Fidel, of El Che, and of all the revolutionary heroes. I want to dance, have a good meal, some drinks, and sex in a nice hotel. What's wrong with that? Isn't that what people do *outside*? I want to feel alive! Look at yourself!" she continued with a passion he had never seen in her before, "a loyal party member, a brilliant heart surgeon, a veteran defending the Nicaraguan socialist government. Who are you today in Cuba? You don't even make enough money to fix your damn Russian refrigerator."

Jorge lowered his eyes. She was right, only dollars opened doors these days, and he didn't have any. Jorge had been in Nicaragua, he was a revolutionary, he was tired and frustrated. He spent all day trying to negotiate a solution for his refrigerator. It was impossible; he didn't have enough money. He would have to put his pride aside and start moonlighting like everyone else. Maybe he could help wait on tables in a *paladar*. He had a friend who had just opened one. Anyway, his refrigerator would have to wait.

The next morning, Jorge was awakened by a knock at the door. Who could it be at 7:30 on a Sunday morning? He opened the door. A young man holding a set of tools in his hands said: "I'm here to fix your old Atlant." Understanding the reason for Jorge's puzzled expression, the young man continued, "and don't worry about anything doctor, we understand your situation. Blanquita has already paid for everything."

Socialism or Death, Socialism or Growth, Growth or Death

Clearly, the reforms were not enacted in a political vacuum. There had been an ongoing debate between the old guard, who feared experimenting with drastic changes during such hard times, and the reformists, who were pushing for more liberalization. But as the economy deteriorated and life for Cubans became unbearable, the time was ripe for new ideas and leadership. The situation had to change, and with it the leadership that had been managing the economy. There was a need for new people and a new discourse. Interestingly, the new people knew the ideological restrictions that surrounded them. A new generation of party leader was given a chance, more profound reforms were implemented, but the socialist orientation had to be maintained.

Carlos Lage, a forty-year-old party leader and the principal architect of the economic reforms, stated in 1993:

> In our Revolution, the ideas are always being renewed and enriched; but the base, the root, the political assumptions, the socialist option chosen by the Cuban people and undertaken by the vast majority, never changes. On the contrary, it consolidates with each renovation.
>
> We have conquered the right to be respected and to be allowed to continue improving our society looking for new values but without giving up those we have conquered.
>
> We are not an economy in transition, nor are our people or our party in transition towards capitalism. We will make the changes that are necessary but we will never make a single concession.

José Luis Rodríguez, the forty-seven-year-old reformist finance and price minister, said in front of the National Assembly in 1994: "In Cuba, there will be no neoliberal adjustment policy, there will not be an honest worker who will see his essential interests affected or sacrificed. We must accept with realism though, that the measures we have to take involve an inevitable quota of sacrifice."

In this complicated balancing act, the reformists knew they had a chance, a window of opportunity they could not let pass by. They took it, and important reforms were instrumented. Unfortunately, in spite of the good will of policymakers, the reforms brought with them undesired social inequities. And intolerance of inequity is perhaps the greatest legacy of socialism among Cubans.

Once the reforms were enacted, those with dollars led a better life than those trapped in the peso economy. For the traditional elites, medical doctors, university professors, and artists whose salaries were in pesos, it was difficult to accept that a self-employed person, "a petty capitalist," made up to fifty times more than they did. There were two Cubas, drifting apart; they lived different lives and craved different futures.

Notes

1. Isaiah Berlin, "On Isaiah Berlin", Michael Ignatieff, *The New York Review of Books,* Vol. XLIV, Number 20, December 1997.
2. Carranza, Gutiérrez y Monreal, *Cuba: La Restructuración de la Economía,* 14.
3. The formal transalation for *jinetear* is "horse-riding." The word has been used for men and women who moonlight in illegal activities such as selling stolen cigars or prostitution.

6

CAPITALISM "A LA CUBANA"

> Today, life, reality . . . forces us to do what we would
> have never done otherwise . . . we must make conces-
> sions.
>
> Fidel Castro
> July 26, 1993[1]

With uncharacteristic humility, Fidel Castro's government began a series of market-oriented reforms designed to increase the production and
supply of goods, attract hard currency, and revalue the Cuban peso.
The most important reforms implemented were the legalization of dollar holdings, the liberalization of services permitting self-employment,
the creation of agricultural cooperatives and the opening of farmers'
markets, the elimination of subsidies, tax reforms, and measures to attract more foreign investment.

Let's Try Again: The Second Wave of Reforms

Most reforms were implemented between July 1993 and December 1994. However, the diverse political and social reactions to them
are still being felt.

The Government Gets Its Share by Legalizing Dollar Holdings

In July 1993, Law-Decree 140 legalized dollar holdings in Cuba.
From then on, for the first time since the Revolution, all Cuban citizens
were free to carry and trade with dollars throughout the country. By
attracting dollars to the formal economy, the government could design
mechanisms to get its share of them. As part of measures to tighten the
embargo on Cuba and foil the Castro government's efforts to get its hands
on dollar income, President Clinton announced on August 20, 1994, a
ban on sending family remittances from the United States to Cuba.

Living with Dollars

Ernesto had been waiting for the bus for an hour and a half when he saw his friend Francisco, who was also late for the Cuban Workers Confederation[2] (CTC) meeting. Three million workers had met at 80,000 CTC local offices in the three months since January, 1994. The purpose of those meetings was to analyze and discuss the recent economic reforms, their social impact, and to make some recommendations to the government at the next session of the National Assembly. One of the most controversial reforms had been the legalization of dollar holdings. Ernesto knew the government wanted to get its hands on those precious black market dollars and encourage families in exile to send more dollars home. As it was, estimates for remittances ranged from US$200 million to US$1 billion.[3] Black markets had acted as a safety valve for unsatisfied demand but had also interfered with the government's control of consumer behavior.

Immediately after legalizing dollar holdings, the government opened dollar stores to the Cuban public in order to attract more hard currency. Before 1989, only the Soviets had been allowed to shop in these stores, which were known as *Diplotiendas*. In the '90s, even though all Cubans were free to shop there, a new form of discrimination was at work; only those with dollars could buy and those without them were angry, very angry. At the National Assembly, the finance minister had tried to explain the deep redistributive objectives of the measure: "Among the measures designed to attract and control hard currency, we have opened a chain of retail stores. The objective is to sell products at very high prices to those who have dollars; then the government will be able to redistribute the margin among those who need it more."[4]

It was a brilliant strategy from the government's point of view, thought Ernesto. With the legalization of the dollar, more remittances were attracted and the high prices at the dollar retail stores acted as a hidden sales tax on those remittances. Ernesto also understood that some services needed to be offered in dollars so they could be spent back in the system—hence the decision to liberalize over 117 services, professions, and self-employment opportunities and open the farmers' market. He understood all this with his head, but his heart was somewhere else. He was angry and frustrated.

For him, all those choices were out of reach. His salary was in pesos; he was working in a state-owned company that was losing a lot of money. Actually, he didn't know how bad they were doing until the numbers were discussed in the CTC meetings. He had discovered that production was very low and there wasn't enough to pay for salaries.

They had to learn to be efficient. That was the government's message. There simply wasn't enough money to keep on subsidizing them or any other of the state's money-losers. For hours, they had been discussing all the changes that were needed. It was called the *decentralization* process. Of all the announced changes, one in particular made a lot of sense to him: the possibility that dollar bonuses would be offered to those with the highest productivity. Some joint ventures were already doing it. Why not them?

Although it all made perfect economic sense, Ernesto felt deep in his heart that something was wrong; there was a paradox, an inversion of revolutionary values. He felt very uncomfortable. Those with the least contact outside the island were worse off. Those with families who continued to work for the revolution were worse off. Those working for the government were worse off. This inversion of the traditional ethical code was difficult to swallow. He couldn't accept it. In spite of what the government said, he knew that the legalization of the dollar, the government retail stores, the farmers' market and the legalization of self-employment were needed reforms, but that they enhanced inequality. He knew that in other places it was called capitalism. So what was left of socialism?

He had watched the differences flourish with the reforms. People with access to dollars had nicer clothes, ate better food, and went to restaurants. He didn't have any family abroad and since he and his wife worked for the government, they had no way of accessing dollars from the tourist industry either.

Francisco, Ernesto's friend from the factory, joined him at the bus stop and asked him a question he dreaded answering. "Ernesto, what are you doing waiting for the bus? What happened to your white Lada?"[5]

"I don't have it anymore and don't ask me anything else," snapped Ernesto, hoping Francisco would drop the subject.

"What do you mean?" Francisco insisted. "Don't tell me you sold it to a *maceta*!"[6] "Haven't you read what the people at the National Assembly are saying about that? Here, read about it!" and he handed Ernesto a copy of *Granma*.

Grabbing the newspaper with his fist, Ernesto launched into his own sermon. "Don't give me an ethical speech in front of all these people. Let me tell you what you already know. Why do I need a car parked on the streets when I don't have any money for gas? Why do I need a car when my family can't go to sleep at night because they're hungry? How could I *not* sell the car? Besides, haven't you noticed? Holding dollars isn't illegal anymore, so what's your problem? I sold it for US$1,000. And *you,* my friend, would have done the same."

Francisco responded to his friend's anger by reading aloud from the newspaper. "Much of yesterday's debate at the meeting of the National Assembly focused on the issue of cars and houses being sold illegally by first class *compañeros,* who had earned them through their work and revolutionary behavior. According to one representative from the district of Cotorro, these *compañeros* are illegally selling cars and houses to macetas in order to get dollars. Specialists forge property documents to make the transaction half-legal. This is an unacceptable situation which must be solved with judicial mechanisms."[7]

He looked up at Ernesto for a moment, then continued reading, punctuating his point with a quote from Fidel himself: "We can not permit these illegal transactions with cars and houses to continue. We will make sure these violations of the law do not go unpunished."[8]

Ernesto knew about this type of criticism. He had been listening to these arguments—and others—for months. He also knew how these messages were supposed to affect him and thousands like him. He was angry because he was afraid. And that's exactly what they wanted. They wanted him to be afraid. So if he knew that, why couldn't he control himself. Everybody in Cuba had done something illegal sometime. Everybody in Cuba during the "special period" had participated in some kind of "unacceptable" behavior; even those who were now pontificating at the National Assembly had succumbed. They'd have to put everybody in jail for violating the law. He didn't worry anymore; but still, he was afraid.

More Services and More Jobs: Authorizing Self-employment

Among other economic reforms in 1993, the Cuban government legalized limited forms of self-employment as a source of jobs and services. Self-employment was aimed both at taking a bite out of growing unemployment and at meeting demand for some goods and services that the state was unable to provide. Goods and services produced by the self-employed could be sold to the population at prices determined only by supply and demand, in pesos or in dollars.

Given the chance to earn their incomes outside the state sector, many Cubans jumped at the opportunity and joined the ranks of the so-called *cuentapropias.* Although self-employment has existed in Cuba in one form or another throughout the revolutionary years, the publication of Law-Decree 141 in September 1993 in which the government published a list of 117 authorized occupations, propelled its expansion. Notably, university professions were not included. The argument was that the state had very generously spent its resources on educating the country's

SEAN SPRAGUE

She'll replace your watch battery — satisfaction guaranteed!

elite in the most important professions. Now it was their turn to return to society what had freely been given to them. Unfortunately, this seemingly winning argument has condemned the best of the Cuban intelligentsia to the worst standard of living.

Self-employment has caused considerable controversy in Cuba since its inception. The government was not—and still isn't—comfortable with a flourishing capitalist enclave of Cubans, yet it relies on self-employment for unemployment relief, tax revenue, and the incorporation of more Cubans into the dollar economy.

> Whereas in the present conditions of the Special Period in which the country's economic activity has been affected by the lack of material resources of various types, it is advisable to expand the sphere of self-employment carried out by persons with the aptitude and the resources for such activity. It is necessary to provide the organization and establish the required order to ensure that self-employment responds to particular principles that favor its development in all areas that are useful to the people, while keeping the practice of it from taking *harmful*[9] forms.[10]

In other words, according to the above description, in the same decree where self-employment is legalized, the regulator justifies the activity in a very restricted context. First, it is closely related to the Special Period. Many Cubans have interpreted this to mean that self-employment is temporary. Also, it is clearly stated that the activity requires important regulation and, finally, that society should be aware that it could take "harmful forms."

More Food and More Jobs: Creating Cooperatives and Farmers' Markets

The organization of agricultural production into big state farms began to collapse in 1989 when the lack of oil, fuel, fertilizers, and spare parts adversely affected the productivity of large-scale, capital-intensive farming. Since capital was scarce, the government decided to stimulate smaller, more labor-intensive farms. Reforms in this sector were thus oriented to changing both a) the organization of production and b) the structure of incentives. The creation of the UBPC (Unidades Básicas de Producción Cooperativa) represented an important change in both aspects.

> Until 1993 the development of the agricultural sector in Cuba was based on State ownership and exploitation of large extensions of land, with high technical development and imported supplies. When the latter had to be reduced, the model needed to be changed.[11]

Essentially, imported supplies had to be replaced by labor. To do this, incentives had to be introduced to attract members of the labor force from other jobs to the farms.

The UBPC were born in September 1993 with the purpose of trans-forming large state farms into cooperatives. Land ownership in Cuban agriculture has experienced three important changes. The first agrarian reform, enacted in May 1959, eliminated large estates of 405 hectares or more and promoted the development of cooperatives. The second agrarian reform, in October 1963, authorized the state to expropriate farms greater than sixty-seven hectares in size and become the owner and manager of more than ninety percent of Cuba's agricultural land. Thirty years later, in September 1993, the Cuban State Council enacted Law-Decree No. 142 establishing the Basic Units of Cooperative Pro-duction on state land with the following principles:

1. UBPCs would have the usufruct of the land for an indefinite period of time. They would not own the land but could share the profits.

2. The cooperative would own what is produced.

3. Salaries would be directly related to productivity.

4. The UBPCs would have managerial autonomy.

TABLE 6.1   The State Cedes Control of the Land

	1992	1996
Total State	75.2	32.6
Total Non-State	24.8	67.4
UBPC	—	42.1
CPA	9.7	9.7
CCS		11.8
Private ownership		3.8

Source: La Economía Cubana en 1996: Resultados, Problemas y Perspectivas. Centro de Estudios de la Economía Cubana (CEEC).

5. The cooperatives could manage bank accounts.

6. The UBPCs could collectively elect their leadership who would periodically report to its members.

With the creation of the UBPCs, the participation of the non-state agricultural sector in the economy grew from 24.8 percent in 1992 to almost seventy percent in 1996. The UBPCs controlled 42.1 percent of the land while the Credit and Service Cooperatives (CCS) occupied 11.8 percent. Agricultural Production Cooperatives (CPA)[12] and private ownership accounted for 9.7 percent.

UBPCs were designed so that producers associated with them didn't have legal ownership of the land. Nevertheless, allowing output and profits to be owned by the members of the cooperative provided an important incentive. Still, there were key problems to be resolved. "We had to sell all production to the government at a set price. In the end, there wasn't much in the way of profits," said a cooperative member.

During that first year, members of the UBPCs complained mainly about the excessive interference of the state and demanded direct access to markets. Actually, the UBPCs copied from other cooperative experiments of the '80s. They were supposed to sell their quota volumes to the state at fixed official prices, and receive a premium for production in excess of their quotas. During the 1980s, this system provided incentives for the cooperatives to produce in excess and sell the extra production to the state. However, the food shortages of the early 1990s and subsequently soaring prices in the black market reduced the incentive to sell excess production—or any production for that matter—to

the state. The state was the only market for the production of the cooperatives from September 1993, when they were created, until farmers'
markets, or *mercados agropecuarios* (MA), began operating in Cuba
after they were legalized by Law-Decree 191 in September 1994.

For many analysts, the decision to reinstate farmers' markets was a
blow to Castro's authority. He had ordered the closing of the *mercados
libres campesinos* (MLC) in the '80s. But the food shortages of the '90s
were about to cause a major political crisis. Following the social unrest
and the rafter crisis in the summer of 1994, Castro was forced to make
concessions once more and the second major change in the agricultural
sector was approved. Nevertheless, there were two major differences
between the free farmers' markets of the '90s and those of the '80s.
Now, state farms were also authorized to sell in the newly created farmers' markets to compete with non-state producers: cooperatives and
private producers, and cooperatives and private farmers were expected
to pay taxes.

Cuatro Caminos: A Farmers' Market in Havana

Supply and demand are the first words you hear upon entering a
Havana free market. There is no electricity, poor ventilation, no fans
and no refrigeration. But under the hot sun at 35 degrees centigrade,
Cubans buy and sell pork, sausages, goats, live hens, vegetables, and
fruits. "The price of pork is now," as a vendor looks at his watch, "28
pesos but, you know, it all depends on supply and demand."

"What does that mean?" someone asks.

"Well, it's simple. If by three o'clock, I haven't sold sixty percent of
this cut of meat, I lower the price, and if by seven o'clock things don't
look good, I'll give a party with whatever is left and you are invited."
Jorge was a medical student and he is now a *representante*; he got a
license to sell at the market. He is eager to explain that he doesn't buy
the meat from the farmers, he sells it *for* them and they share the profits.

Pedro is the farmer; he has always worked at the farm. He is fifty-
five years old and is afraid and ashamed to speak. He raises pigs. He
has always worked the land; it is his land. He was ten years old when
his father got the piece of land he still works on. He does not sell directly to the consumer; his responsibility is to slaughter the animals and
transport them from the farm to the market by truck. "I pay the owner
of the truck; he also has a license to be self-employed; he also has to pay
taxes." The owner of the truck used to work for the government, now
his job is to transport pork and other products to the market. He got

the truck by trading his old car to a friend working in a cooperative. The farmer refuses to say how much money he is making. Profit is not a popular word in Cuba these days. The self-employed, "*cuenta propias*" or "*no asalariados*," were being harshly criticized by those who earn salaries in pesos. "They say we are selfish and unscrupulous. We say they are envious."

The farmer insists that he does not do the selling. It is Jorge, a thin but muscular twenty-year-old with inquisitive eyes who does the selling "and the cutting, so what?" he says defiantly. He learned to cut meat from an uncle, and he carries a bag with his utensils: three big knives, a huge sharpener, and a glove made out of a kind of steel thread for his left hand, so he doesn't get hurt. He cuts with great skill. Jorge was a medical student until he decided to quit and become a farmer's agent, or a *representante*. He is responsible for preparing the various cuts of pork and dealing with the clients. He carries the risk of the *cut meat*; he is responsible for pricing and selling it. He pays the taxes and the rent; he is also "in charge of the numbers" and uses a calculator all the time.

"I quit medical school because the state doesn't have a job for me anymore. I had good grades and was accepted to medical school but on a physician's salary I couldn't lead a decent life." He is sick and tired of paying taxes to the government. "I might have to go out of business soon because taxes are so high. They don't know what they're doing." Jorge has to pay five percent of his daily sales in taxes, plus 200 pesos a month, 125 pesos per day for the rent of the stand, and an annual tax, the amount of which they haven't decided upon yet.

Jorge is one of Cuba's new capitalists but, defying the stereotype, his greed has its limits. An elderly woman approaches the counter, inquires about the price of the pork chops, and starts complaining. When she finishes her tirade, he gives her a pound for free. "There you go *compañera*. Please accept this, no charge. I know how you feel. My mother would have said the same, but you know, it's not my fault, it's that socialism, just didn't work." She takes the chops and thanks him.

"This is a special type of capitalism. We don't cut throats here. We respect those who have given the best years of their life for the revolution." Jorge is the "*representante*," a new word allowed by the government to avoid the use of the word "intermediary," or middle man, which carries a stigma from former attempts at liberalization. The *representante* sells and pays the farmer his share, 20 pesos per pound, of what they sold during the day. What is not sold and uncut, the farmer takes away. The unsold cut meat is the risk run by the *representante*. Jorge works twelve hours a day, seven days a week, and says he would like to make more money and get married someday. He lives with his mother, who is not working anymore. She is retired and gets 120 pesos a month (less than US$4) for her pension. Life is tough, very tough, but Jorge sings a well-known Mexican song: "*con dinero y sin dinero, hago siempre lo que quiero.*" (With or without money, I do what I please.) Somebody eggs him on by continuing the song, "*y mi palabra es la ley*" (and my word is the law). He laughs, "that part I leave to Fidel."

Around the corner in the same market Alexandra, a chemical engineer, works for a cooperative and sells sweet potatoes at three pesos per pound. She is angry because state companies are pushing the price down. "This isn't fair. They don't have to pay taxes, they don't have to make money for a living. They get their salaries no matter what. They come here just to bother us." She talks with both hands on her hips—loud, defiant, smiling, and turning once in a while to check who's listening. "Here, nobody pretends to be private and when you speak you know there is always somebody listening. This is not life. I want to get out of here, the heat, the smell. I went to school and studied hard, for what? To sell potatoes?" She is waiting to be called for a job at the *Base Area de Combate*. "They'll open it soon," she says with a smile and without much hope. In her new job, if she ever gets it, she will get rid of the smell and the heat but not the misery; she will be making 240 pesos.

Increasing Taxes and Eliminating Subsidies: Is This Capitalism or What?

"We had the money to do what we did, we even had the money to subsidize those who got used to subsidies, but under the current situation, we cannot escape the need to impose taxes, a policy which is also oriented to clean up our internal finances."[13]

Eusebio had to leave the smoke-filled room for a while. Cigars were the only abundant commodity in Cuba those days. He had been working at the Finance and Price Ministry for the past two years. He knew how difficult the coming session at the National Assembly would be for the minister. The long hours preparing his presentation to the delegates had been endless.

Even after all the controversial reforms in 1993, by 1994 the government needed to reduce the cash imbalances and excess liquidity. Liquidity (pesos in the hands of Cubans) had soared from 4.9 billion pesos in 1990 to over eleven billion pesos by the end of 1993. Of course, the concept of excess liquidity is relative. The question "excess compared to what" is the answer the minister had to provide in order to persuade the members of the National Assembly that a reduction in

TABLE 6.2   The Government Was Broke But It Kept Spending:
Cash in Circulation (millions of pesos)

	1990	1991	1992	1993
Total year end	4, 986	6, 663	8, 361	11, 043
% of GDP	23.9	38.0	51.0	66.5

Source: La Economía Cubana, Reformas Estructurales y Desempeño en los Noventa, 1997. ECLAC. Fondo de Cultura Economica, Mexico, 1997.

government expenses was absolutely necessary. There was also an urgent need to increase government income. According to some government calculations, the necessary money supply was estimated at 3.5 billion pesos.[14] Excess liquidity is particularly easy to estimate in socialist economies because the state provides most of the goods and services. There is no monetary policy; governments just print the money they need and there are no complicated financial systems. The Cuban government was broke, it had been paying for more commitments than it could afford (salaries, social programs, and the *libreta*). The government needed to explicitly default on them, or liquidity would continue growing.

Eusebio and the rest of the minister's team had made the calculations. The next reforms had to include a drastic cutback in subsidies, an increase in a wide variety of prices, higher rates for water and electricity, and some kind of new taxes, preferably on income. Not very good news, indeed.

The political situation had been deteriorating, especially after the legalization of dollar holdings. Given the scarcity of hard currency, the government strategy had been to attract dollars not only from foreign investment, but from Miami as well. Many in the party leadership with no ties and no families in exile, couldn't accept that after having bet everything they had on the revolution, they had ended up in a worse situation than those who had left.

Eusebio remembered the painful conversation with his eighteen-year-old nephew who had decided to build a raft and try his luck at sea. If the message from the government was, the more dollars the better, "let me go to Miami," he had said, "there are more dollars there." His nephew had left a month ago. He hadn't come back, he hadn't sent dollars, he hadn't arrived to Miami—there wasn't a trace. For obvious reasons, the legalization of the dollar had inspired heated criticism.

In spite of the reforms implemented to boost the supply of goods,

ANA JULIA JATAR-HAUSMANN

They're off to sea on inner tubes. But are they going fishing or going to Miami?

the excess liquidity problem had not been solved. The process of adjustment in Cuba had been carried out while trying to avoid any social hardship. Employment was maintained by subsidizing enterprises. And programs in health, education, and social security were not reduced in order to maintain political consensus for the reforms. While the government kept up its spending, the costs of the adjustment program showed up as excess liquidity and money supply. The reforms to increase production were right, but the liquidity problem had gotten out of hand and was impeding economic recovery.

The most damaging effects of excess liquidity were:

1. The growth of the black market
2. The decline in labor productivity
3. Inflation in the black market, where people increasingly shopped
4. The depreciation of the peso and, therefore, wages

Eusebio had been crunching numbers for many months. The National Assembly will have to choose between two options to attack the liquidity problem: A monetary reform to create a new currency with an important degree of expropriation; or a program of demonetization. In

other words, a set of unpopular measures to reduce the number of pesos in circulation, which would lead to an acceptable level of liquidity.
None of the options was politically attractive.

The minister was prepared to present the different options to reduce the fiscal deficit by the end of 1994. The menu of options included:

1. Reducing subsidies to state enterprises

2. Increasing the prices of cigarettes, gasoline, and alcohol

3. Raising rates for water, electricity, transportation, and postal
    services

4. Charging for cultural and sports events

5. Charging for a small number of medicines

6. Increasing taxes on private farmers and cooperatives

7. Designing a tax for dollar incomes (excluding remittances)

8. Implementing a system of workers' contributions to social se-
    curity

9. Raising taxes on the self-employed

The government was also prepared to implement a monetary reform, should the National Assembly approve it.[15]

In the end, the National Assembly decided against monetary reform and backed the government in implementing a set of unpopular
measures to reduce the fiscal deficit. The government had to get the
fiscal deficit under control soon. It was going to be painful, but there
was no alternative.

In May 1994, the National Assembly authorized the government to
do the following:

1. Systematically reduce the subsidy to state enterprises

2. Achieve the stability of savings deposits at the Popular Bank of
    Savings (BPA)

3. Define appropriate measures to stimulate production in order
    to rapidly increase the supply of goods and services to the popu-
    lation

4. Evaluate the possibility of raising the prices of selected goods
    as well as taxes and rates on items such as cigarettes, alcohol,
    electricity, water, and others

5. Design and implement a socially sensitive tax system that would
    protect people in the lower-income brackets. It should also

stimulate work and production in order to contribute to resolving the nation's financial problems. The system must selectively introduce a personal income tax, but not on salaries.

6. Evaluate the possibility of a monetary reform (i.e., devaluation) to complement the fiscal reform

7. Implement other policies that would contribute to improving the country's financial situation

Not surprisingly, these policies inspired a contentious debate at the National Assembly. Tax reforms were a particularly bitter pill to swallow. Almost thirty years after Cuba abolished personal income taxes as being irrelevant to a communist society, confusion reigns over what its re-adoption really means.

The government had no choice but to expand its sources of income while it reduced subsidies and salaries. On the income side, taxes were increased by twenty-four percent. A new income tax was imposed on the self-employed, farmers, and cooperativists. There was a substantial increase in prices of some goods and services such as tobacco, liquor, water, electricity, transportation, gas, and postal services, among others. On the expenditures side, a reduction of nine percent was achieved by drastically cutting the size of the central government: fifteen ministries were eliminated and many subsidies in education and health were reduced. A social security contribution of up to twelve percent of wages was introduced in early 1995 to pay for the country's onerous pensions.

It took more than two years for the members of the National Assembly to agree on the need to reinstate taxes. The debate, long known to capitalist societies, is still in its infancy in Cuba. The authorities now tax all hard currency income except remittances sent from abroad. Peso salaries remain untaxed. As liberal as they may seem to some, the reforms adopted to date are not enough, and some high Cuban government officials agree that a more comprehensive tax reform is needed in the future. In 1996, the self-employed paid 200 million pesos in taxes, accounting for 1.6 percent of all government revenues. Obviously, the political viability of this policy will depend on the development of a profitable private sector. The size to which this private sector should be allowed to grow is also a source of debate. In the meantime, the private sector has reacted violently.

More Hard Currency and New Technology: Courting Foreign Investors

Before 1989, the Soviet Union provided Cuba with the hard currency, the technology, and the markets it needed to support the economy. Now, the Cuban government relies heavily on foreign investment for such purposes. For this reason, it is actively courting new investors and seducing them into making major financial commitments. However, this time around Cuba isn't looking for a steady partner to depend on. Instead, it's committed to playing the field: "We went to bed one night and when we woke up, the Soviet Union was not there anymore and we had to begin all over again. The same thing had occurred years before with the United States. This is not going to happen again to us."[16]

If the Cuban government has shown a firm commitment to anything since the beginning of the crisis, it has been to attracting as many countries as possible to bring their dollars to Cuba. Different sources suggest that foreign investment agreements totaling about US$2 billion—through the year 2005—have been signed between the Cuban government and nineteen countries including Australia, Canada, France, Germany, Great Britain, Israel, Italy, Mexico, Spain, and others.

Originally, the intention was to attract foreign investment only in tourism. This was viewed as the safest way to keep the capitalist experiment under control. Reality, however, forced the government to open other sectors to private capital as it searched for new technologies and hard currency. Castro himself accepted the new reality and the impact of having to adjust to life without Soviet aid. He said in 1993: "Who would have thought that we, so doctrinaire, who fought foreign investment, would one day view foreign investment as an urgent need?"[17]

The most widely opened sectors behind tourism are agriculture (mainly tobacco and citrus), mining (nickel, lead, gold, and chrome), oil and coal, telecommunications, and textiles.

To lure new investors, Cuba has signed investment protection agreements with most investor countries guaranteeing equal treatment, abstention from nationalization, and the right to repatriate profits and capital. With the goal of attracting more private capital, the new foreign investment law allows one-hundred percent private foreign ownership. It also permits investment in real estate and the creation of free trade and export manufacturing zones. Discussions in the National Assembly over the Foreign Investment Law were heated. The two most controversial features of the bill were to allow Cuban exiles to invest in Cuba with the same rights as other foreign investors and to allow foreign companies to hire employees directly. Only the measure concerning the investment rights of exiles was approved, although changes may be

TABLE 6.3   **Pulling GDP Out of the Ditch**

	1990	1991	1992	1993	1994	1995	1996	1997	1998
GDP %	–2.9	–10.7	–11.6	–14.9	0.7	2.5	7.8	2.5	2.0*

*Expected.
Sources: La Economía Cubana, Reformas Estructurales y Desempeño en los Noventa, 1997. ECLAC. Fondo de Cultura Economica, Mexico, 1997; and Informe Economico, Banco Nacional de Cuba, Havana, Cuba.

FIGURE 6.3   **Pulling GDP Out of the Ditch**

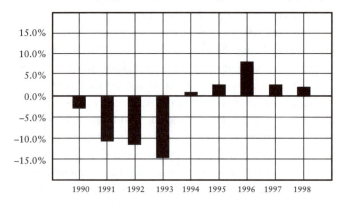

forthcoming in response to growing criticism from abroad. Except in special free trade zones, foreign companies can only hire Cuban workers through a government agency, ACOREC, which assigns workers according to their individual qualifications and pockets the dollar salary, paying employees in pesos. With the official exchange rate still pegged at one peso per US$, workers consider this policy sheer robbery. They wouldn't mind paying the twenty percent income tax if they could exchange their dollars at the unofficial exchange rate. Since they can't, workers consider the income tax an insult, especially after the government opened exchange houses where they were allowed to buy back their dollars, but at the unofficial rate.

By 1996 It Was Clear: The Second Wave of Reforms Was Working

Once the waters had settled following the second wave of reforms, the Cuban economy began to recover. After suffering a forty percent decline in GDP in the 1989–93 period, the economy bottomed out and

TABLE 6.4   Immediate Reaction to the Reforms: Growth of Exports

(millions of US $)	Cuban Exports Selected Data			
	1993	1994	1995	1996
Nickel	120	130	260	338
Tobacco	80	85	95	125
Medical Products	20	120	120	134
Fishing	90	110	110	133

Source: CIA and Cuban Government.

has been recuperating ever since. After timid growth of 0.7 percent in 1994 and 2.5 percent in 1995, GDP grew 7.8 percent in 1996 and 2.5% in 1997 and about the same was expected for 1998.

According to the 1994 Economic ECLAC report, more than eighteen industrial sectors grew during the 1993–96 period including nickel, oil, citrus, textiles, construction, fishing, and others. For the first time, tourism displaced sugar as the principal source of foreign exchange, providing US$850 million in 1994, or thirty-five percent of Cuba's total dollar revenue, and US$1.38 billion in 1996, more than forty percent of dollar revenues for that year. Evidently, the economy adjusted to a lower level of activity. GNP stopped contracting in 1994 thanks to the expansion of new activities such as tourism, mining, oil, and non-sugar manufacturing. Foreign investment in these new activities had also been growing.

Hoping that foreign investment alone would turn the economy around had not worked. When a different set of reforms was implemented, using dollars from remittances and tourists to fuel the economy, the recovery was immediate. By 1996, almost forty percent of Cuba's total dollar income and sixty-five percent of exports were coming from tourists visiting the island and dollars sent home by families abroad. According to estimates, US$1.38 billion dollars were coming to the island as gross tourist revenue and US$820 million dollars as remittances. Total dollar exports were US$3,380 million. "Private transfers," in other words money sent home by expatriots, have increasingly replaced "Official transfers," or Soviet Aid (see Table 6.5). Also, the strategy of "exporting" to Cubans within Cuba by permitting them to buy in dollars allowed for a further increase in goods and services exports.

This strategy also allowed Cuba to become less dependent on sugar

TABLE 6.5 Balance of Payments: Selected Figures
Tourists and Exiles Begin to Pay for Imports

(million of US$)	1989	1990	1991	1992	1993	1994	1995	1996	1997[d]
Total Exports	5,993	5,940	3,563	2,522	1,992	2,247	2,687	3,380	3,932
Goods	5,392	5,415	2,980	1,779	1,137	1,315	1,479	1,976	1,860
Services[c]	601	525	583	743	855	932	1208	1,413	2,072
Imports	8,606	8,017	4,702	2,737	2,373	2,408	3,187	4,462	5,400
Trade Balance	−2,615	−2,077	−1,139	−215	−381	−161	−500	−1,082	−1,468
Official Transfers[a]	3,000	1,000	500	50	50	—	—	—	—
Private Transfers[b]	20	50	100	200	315	529	600	820	900

a. Soviet aid.   b. Mainly remittances from exile.   c. Includes tourism and other local services (self-employment) paid in U.S. dollars.
d. Approximate figures subject to change.
Sources: See ECLAC, Cuba: Evolución Económica 1995, La Economía Cubana: Reformas Estructurales y Desempeño de los Noventa, Anexo Estadístico, CEPAL, Agosto, 1997. Banco Nacional de Cuba, Informe Economico 1996. Informe Económico año 1997. Ministerio de la Economía y Planificación. Habana, Cuba.

for production and exports. Cuba has an important competitive advantage in tourism, which since 1994 has replaced sugar as the number one hard currency producer in the country.

The steady increase in economic output combined with fiscal and tax reform brought the fiscal deficit down. After reaching –30 percent of GDP in 1993, the deficit was trimmed to only –2.3 percent of GDP in 1996.

The reforms also brought a measure of control over liquidity and as soon as the fiscal deficit began to subside, liquidity growth could be tamed. From sixty-seven percent of GDP in 1993, liquidity reached only thirty-seven percent in 1996.

Another favorable economic sign during the 1993–96 period was the recovery of the peso. After reaching 150 pesos per dollar in 1993, the exchange rate began to fall until it stabilized at around 22 pesos per dollar in December 1996. By 1998 it was 20 pesos per dollar. Despite the marked improvement, the situation is still far from stable. Huge distortions generated by the gap between the official and unofficial rates have caused major inefficiencies in the allocation of resources. For example, since income in dollars represents twenty-two times more than income in pesos, there has been a mass exodus of university professionals to less skilled activities that provide dollar remuneration.

Capitalism "a la Cubana": Dealing with New Partners

The flourishing dollar economy has brought a new life for many Cubans. For those still trapped in the peso economy, especially government employees, it is the end of the revolution, despite Fidel's message to the contrary.

> It has shattered the carefully calibrated egalitarianism of Cuba's society during the Soviet bloc years, which was built on a uniform national food rationing system and subsidized prices. Privileged groups, mostly linked to the hierarchy of political power, did exist but the basic relationship between wages, income and prices was the same for the majority of citizens.[18]

In spite of the complex social and political circumstances, there was a new sense of hope in the air in 1996. New reforms were imminent and everyone hoped the changes would increasingly bring the two Cubas together. But there was also a fear, it had happened before: a backlash.

A new generation of Cubans that missed the heady days of the revolution is beginning to taste the fruits of market-oriented reforms. Having

TABLE 6.6   The Changing Roles of Sugar and Tourism (millions of US$ and thousands of tourists)

	1990	1991	1992	1993	1994	1995	1996	1997	1998 (e)
Sugar Exports	4,316	2,261	1,221	752	748	704	951	900	
Tourism gross Earnings	242	387	567	720	850	1,100	1,380	1,500	1,800
No. of Tourists (.000)	340	424	461	546	617	745	990	1,169	1,400

Sources: CIA and Informe Económico, Banco Nacional de Cuba, 1996.

TABLE 6.7 The Rise and Fall of the Fiscal Deficit

	1989	1990	1991	1992	1993	1994	1995	1996	1997
Fiscal Income	12, 501	12, 225	10, 949	9, 262	9, 515	12, 756	11, 593	12, 124	
Fiscal Expenditure	12, 904	14, 213	14, 713	14, 131	14, 566	14, 178	12, 368	12, 692	
Fiscal Deficit	−1, 403	−1, 958	−3, 764	−4, 869	−5, 050	−1, 421	−765.5	−568	−450
Fiscal Def. % GDP	−6.7	−9.4	−21.4	−29.7	−30.5	−6.9	−3.2	−2.3	−2.0

Sources: ECLAC, La Economía Cubana, 1997; Banco National de Cuba, 1996; Informe Económico del Año 1997. Ministerio de Economía y Planificación. Havana, Cuba.

This bicycle repair man has his own private business on a very public street.

whet their appetite, they are pressing for more. If the formula of the past is to be repeated, the time is ripe for a backlash against these market-oriented tendencies. However, the Cuba of the '90s is not the Cuba of the '80s. In the '80s, economic openings were attempts to ameliorate the systemic scarcity, inefficient investments, and widespread waste that

TABLE 6.8   Controlling Liquidity Growth

	1993	1994	1995	1996	1997
Pesos in Circulation	11, 043	9,943	9, 251	9,534	9, 441
Percentage of GDP	67	48	39	37	35

Sources: ECLAC: La Economia Cubana 1997; Informe Económico del Año 1997; Ministerio de Economía y Planificación, Havana, Cuba.

TABLE 6.9   Closing the Exchange Rate Gap

	1993	1994	1995	1996	1997
Official exchange rate	1	1	1	1	1
Unofficial exchange rate	100	130	35	22	20

Source: Informe Económico, Banco Nacional de Cuba, Cuba News, January 1998.

typically plague centrally planned economies. Cuban officials experimented with the reforms, but they never had a major impact on the underlying structure of the economy. Cuba was highly dependent on Soviet rent; it could pay for the socialist backlash and more.

That security blanket is no longer there. Instead of the Soviets, the Cuban government has four new partners: foreign investors, Cuban exiles, tourists, and an emerging private sector. These are the new actors and the new constituency for the reforms.

With the help of these four partners, capitalism is emerging through the cracks of socialism. The challenge for Cubans today is to resolve the tensions generated by the intrinsic contradictions between the two systems. The future of the economy and the welfare of Cubans depend on how these contradictions get resolved.

Notes

1. Fidel Castro, Speech at the National Assembly, July 26, 1993, Havana, Cuba. Foreign Broadcasting International Service: FBIS-LAT-93-143, Daily Report, July 27, 1993, Vol. VI, Number 142.
2. Conferederación de Trabajadores Cubanos.
3. González Núñez, "La Economia Cubana."
4. José Luis Rodríguez, Asamblea Nacional del Poder Popular, 1994. *Debates en el Parlamento Cubano, 1994.*
5. The Russian car maker.

6. Those who accumulated important quantities of dollars by trading in the black market and by receiving remittances.
7. Asamblea Nacional del Poder Popular, *Debates y Decisiones del Gobierno Cubano*, May, 1994.
8. Asamblea Nacional del Poder Popular.
9. Emphasis by author.
10. *Gazeta Oficial de la Republica de Cuba*, Numero 5, Extraordinaria, 1993.
11. *La Economia Cubana en 1996: Resultados y Perspectivas*, Centro de Estudios de la Economia Cubana (CEEC), Universidad de la Habana, 1997, 77.
12. The main difference between the UBPCs and the CPAs is that the members of the latter own their land while the UBPCs don't.
13. Ricardo Alarcón, President of the National Assembly.
14. *Granma*, interview with José Luis Rodríguez, finance and price minister, Havana, November, 1994.
15. Asamblea Nacional del Poder Popular, *Debates y Decisiones del Parlamento Cubano*, May, 1994.
16. Conversation with the minister of Basic Industries, Portal 1995.
17. Fidel Castro, Speech, July 26, 1993.
18. Pascal Fletcher, *Financial Times*, June, 1997.

7

A Portrait of the Self-Employed: Cuba's Landrafters

> The great dynamic success of capitalism had given us a powerful weapon in our battle against Communism: money.
>
> Ronald Reagan, 1990[1]

For Clara, opening a small restaurant in her tiny house facing the Havana *Malecon,* has been a source of hope and dollars. With this *paladar,*[2] she now makes in a month almost ninety times what she used to earn as an accountant in a government agency. Clara explains convincingly, "The worst is over. We were starving, but things are much better now. People are happier, don't you see?" She points at a couple of Cubans talking and laughing while eating rice, beans, pork, and drinking a local beer. "Finally we have the chance to have a night out." Sitting at other tables, Italian, Spanish, and German tourists seem to enjoy the local cuisine. Clara buys most of the food she needs for her US$4.00 menu at the farmers' markets. Like many other Cubans, Clara enjoys the novelty of buying shoes at the free artisans' market, and dresses, detergent, and olive oil in dollar specialty stores.

José Luis is eighteen years old. He makes wooden statues out of pieces of mahogany he finds in collapsed buildings. He sells them to tourists in the artisans' market near the Cathedral, but he doesn't want to study art. He wants to be important; he wants to be a doctor. His excellent grades in high school have almost guaranteed him a place in medical school next year: "I still have to do very well on the admission test. You know, to be a doctor, you need to be the best." José Luis earns around US$200 a month selling statues—much more than the salary of a medical doctor.

Baster is twenty-seven years old. He has a degree in physical education. He used to teach gymnastics in a high school in Havana. Since

ANA JULIA JATAR-HAUSMANN

Being able to run a small business like this paladar *has expanded the menu of employment options open to Cubans.*

1995, he has worked as the chauffeur and bodyguard of one of the most prominent foreign investors in Cuba. "Life is good now. My wife works in a hotel, she has a good salary, and I have a great job. We can't complain."

Clara, José Luis, and Baster are some of the new actors in the Cuban economy and are part of a growing constituency in favor of reform. Foreign investors, the self-employed, managers, and tourists are changing the face of socialist Cuba. Though not yet the majority, there are a growing number of workers engaged in economic activities that did not even exist in 1993. According to government officials, nearly thirty percent of the labor force is working in market-related activities, in other words, out of the socialist scheme. There are approximately 500,000 Cubans working in self-employed activities. Another half million are receiving dollar or peso incentives from government enterprises or joint ventures, and thousands are earning dollars in activities related to the tourism industry. And the numbers are apt to grow. The huge spread between the official and unofficial exchange rate is pushing the government to incorporate more Cubans into the dollar economy.

Some of the most controversial new actors on the economic scene and a growing constituency in favor of more economic liberalization are the self-employed, or so-called *cuentapropias*. When 117 occupations were liberalized, opening up a whole range of jobs outside the government, many jumped at the chance to set up their own businesses. However, Cubans' limited access to capital and ownership has prevented self-employment from growing beyond a very small scale. For ideological reasons related to the role of a private sector in a socialist society, the economic reforms have raised questions—and more than a few eyebrows—about whether the emergence of a strong private sector would deepen the already growing inequalities in Cuban society. For an egalitarian society in which income disparities were minimized during thirty-five years of socialism, accepting the inequalities that come with capitalism has been ethically difficult. Policies that imply inequities among Cubans have been the target of strong resistance and criticism. According to the new investment law, Cubans in exile have the same legal treatment as other foreign investors. In other words, they are allowed to invest like any other foreign investor. This decision caused heated debate in the National Assembly. The debate is still raging among Cubans over whether private property should be recognized, whether Cubans should be able to hire other Cubans (only the state and foreign investors with government authorization can do so), and whether private services in the form of self-employment should be accepted.

Long debates in the National Assembly have echoed some of the questions Cubans have been asking themselves. The following are some of the arguments for and against self-employment extracted from the discussion at the National Assembly on December 28, 1993.[3]

Arguments in Favor of the Self-employed

- "It is a complement to the State."
- "It is a good job alternative for the unemployed."
- "It will satisfy needs and supply goods and services that are not provided by the state."
- "The government gains control by legalizing and regulating widespread illegal activities." For example, "there are hundreds of illegal food vendors in spite of the prohibitions."
- The state can collect taxes: "now we have the worst situation: there are illegal activities everywhere and the state is not benefiting from them. If we legalize, we control."
- "It is a popular decree; people like it." "It would be very sad if the members of the National Assembly who are supposed to represent the people decide against something that the people want."

Arguments Against the Self-employed:

- Profiteering: "people will be selling at high prices what has been produced by others." "People will be selling products with subsidized inputs or with stolen supplies from state enterprises."

- "Small business will not take us anywhere. It would have been better to create cooperatives." Fidel disagreed, reminding the Assembly of the negative experiences of some cooperatives in the Soviet Union: "we can not turn everything into cooperatives," he said.

- "It may become such an attractive job alternative that it may compete and create labor shortages for state enterprises."

- "It can generate deformities in the system. Minuscule businesses are not the answer, they are neither socialism nor big capitalism." "If we are going to copy capitalism, why does it have to be from poor countries?" "Let's have big companies, not small self-employed."

In spite of the opposition, poor wages in the state sector have pushed many skilled workers into self-employment. Havana is full of engineers driving forty-year-old taxis, psychologists fixing bicycle tires, economists moonlighting as prostitutes, and physicians working as artisans. This small private sector is developing in a colloidal socialist-capitalist environment saturated with inefficiencies and inconsistencies making their challenges and opportunities unique.

For those who have joined the group of *cuentapropias,* the experience is a source of hope and dollars; but for the majority of Cubans with peso salaries, the liberalized professions are responsible for growing inequalities. The political and social impact of this sector is still being felt in Cuba and its future is still being debated. Who are these people? What are their major challenges? Will they survive?

Political Challenge and Economic Hope

Among other market-oriented reforms, in 1993 the Cuban government legalized limited forms of self-employment. For reasons that range from simple curiosity to elaborate ideological arguments, the self-employed sector in Cuba has been extremely successful in attracting the attention of economists, reporters, tourists, and politicians. Despised by traditional elites, the self-employed represent the only private legal entrepreneurial activity in Cuba. For many it has been a source for jobs and economic hope. For others, especially for those who prefer centralized control, this island of capitalism has become a political threat. While much has been written about this capitalist experiment in Cuba, very little information is available on the characteristics of the self-employed. This chapter is an attempt to begin sketching these out. Who are the self-employed? How well educated are they? How do they compare with the general population? What are their major problems and constraints? What are their achievements? How hard do they work? What are their complaints? What makes them happy? The data presented here is the result of many interviews and a survey conducted by the author in different markets in Havana during March and April 1997. During this time, 218 people were interviewed in four farmers' markets, three major artisans markets, and *paladares* or family-owned restaurants. Taxi drivers (in cars and bicycles) and a variety of independently run self-employed businesses were also interviewed. The sample was selected at random and includes people engaged in different activities and from different sectors of Havana. Because of the errors in the data collected, only 196 questionnaires were processed. Although this is a small sample for the purposes of strong statistical influences, it paints a relatively clear picture and provides some answers to these many questions.

Law-Decree 141, September 8, 1993
Selected Articles

Who can be self-employed?

- Workers assigned to work centers, including graduates from middle level technical schools. Leaders are excluded.

- Persons who have been retired for whatever reason, as well as those who have reduced working ability

- Housewives

- University graduates are not authorized to engage in self-employment. All doctors, dentists, teachers, professors, and researchers will have a job guaranteed by the state.[a] So will all other university graduates.

Requirements/conditions for
engaging in self-employment

- The citizen must be registered as being self-employed
- The authorized person must carry out the activity *without employing salaried workers*
- Direct sale to the population of products or services provided by these workers is allowed. An attempt should be made to *prevent at all costs the emergence of intermediaries or parasites* who make profits and enrich themselves by the efforts of others.
- Prices and conditions, as a rule, will be agreed upon by the seller and the purchaser. In case of abuse or of clearly excessive profits, prices may be regulated by the People's Council.
- The state must not withdraw from any activity because of the emergence of self-employment. This activity must be seen as a *complement* to state efforts.
- No progressive tax will be levied since that process is considered to be too complex for this first phase of self-employment; the application of that tax in the future is not ruled out. (This was changed in 1996 when a progressive income tax was introduced with the objective of reducing income inequality.)
- The amount of the monthly fee to be paid will be determined by the municipal administration council, based on a minimum quota set for each occupation.[b]

Box notes

a. This shows how Cuban government officials regard self-employment as a second best alternative to job opportunities in the state sector.
b. A total of 117 activities were listed with minimum quotas ranging from zero (no tax) to 60 pesos per month.

Playing Hide and Seek with the Government

Despite the ongoing ideological debate over the ideal size of the private sector and growing suspicion among some communist leaders, the regulations have been changed so more people can join the sector and the number of authorized activities has been expanded. But what the Cuban government gives with one hand, it takes with the other. The economic success of these small businesses and the growing discontent from those trapped in the peso economy has induced the government to impose more taxes and regulations.

The tensions generated by this situation have led the government to alternately encourage and repress the sector, which in turn has resulted in fluctuations in the numbers of self-employed Cubans. However, these fluctuations reflect the ebb and flow of workers from legality to illegality rather than changes in the absolute number of people entering or leaving the sector for good. The swing from legal to illegal status depends on the relative incentives offered by the government. "If they keep increasing taxes and harassing me the way they are doing I am going to have to go under again," is the common complaint.

The initial reaction to the liberalization of services was impressive. By December 1993, just a few months after its legalization, 70,000 Cubans had obtained licenses for self-employment. In February 1994, however, the government acted to control the burgeoning sector by issuing a list of infractions—including working in unauthorized activities and hiring middlemen—punishable by fines of up to 1,500 pesos. According to various sources, the sector continued to expand rapidly and numbered between 110,000 and 160,000 by December 1994. Another 80,000 Cubans who join the labor force every year would consider self-employment as an option. By the end of 1995, the number of Cubans with self-employment permits reached approximately 208,000 workers, over five percent of the island's four-million-person labor force. According to some official estimates, another 200,000 are working in similar activities but without licenses. On April 24, 1996, Pedro Ross, President of the Cuban Workers Union, acknowledged in a press conference that 100,000 people had been laid off by state industries due to budget cuts. He also said the self-employment sector could absorb three times the current 200,000 people with licenses to "work on their own account."[4]

In June 1996, the Government opened forty new activities for self-employment and increased the monthly flat tax fee for them. The range of fees established in 1993 went from a minimum of zero (exempted) to a maximum of 80 pesos per month, to a new range of 10 to 400 pesos per month. The most successful activities have been taxed with the highest fees. Also, university graduates—previously banned from participating in any self-employed activity—are now allowed to do so. Unfortunately, they are restricted to the 157 legalized activities and may not be self-employed in their field. In other words, professionals

TABLE 7.1   Tax for the Self-employed: Selected Authorized Activities (monthly flat fee in Cuban pesos)

Activity	1993	1996
Artisan	45	200
Taxi Driver	40	100
Food & Beverage Stand	not authorized	400
Shoe producer/seller	45	200
Art restoration	not authorized	100
Baby sitting	exempt	10
Tax collector	non existent	40
Plumber	40	80
Electrician	45	45

Source: Resolución Conjunta No. 1, Ministerios del Trabajo y Finanzas, June 1996, Habana, Cuba.

TABLE 7.2   Registered Self-employment

	December 1994	December 1995	March 1996	January 1998
Total Applications	248,552	390,759	439,368	268,295
Approved and Registered	169,098	208,786	206,824	159,506

Source: Ministerio del Trabajo y Seguridad Social, Habana, Cuba.

are not allowed to moonlight in their own specialties.

After an impressive initial boom, the number of self-employed workers with licenses declined, mainly in response to the imposition of new taxes, in particular, the recently created progressive income tax. Constant harassment and criticism were also contributing factors. Many complained of inspectors dropping by their points of sale or their homes—day and night—asking a myriad of questions with the clear intention of uncovering some sort of wrongdoing. As one *paladar* owner explained: "They come either to check whether the licenses are correct, or whether the people working are acceptable, if they are family members, or if the *paladares* have more than the maximum-allowed twelve chairs. Anything is a good excuse."

Official figures show that the number of self-employed workers fell from 208,824 in March 1996 to 159,506 in January 1998. What is happening? Has the novelty of self-employment run out?

Probably not. People are not leaving the sector; they are going underground and working illegally. Tax reform is perceived by the sector as another manifestation of the government's obsession with control. "Now all the self-employed workers will have to pay taxes. We are not working for the rich," said Castro to the National Assembly in December 1995.

Who Are These Guys Anyway?

Ana Julia had just finished processing the data of 218 questionnaires in her survey; 218 self-employed people interviewed in different markets in Havana. Not bad, but she knew the small size of her sample would be criticized. Still, she remembered her friends back in Washington. "How are you going to do a survey in Cuba? How are you going to go around asking everyone questions without getting in trouble with the authorities?" She didn't have any problems but she didn't want to push her luck either. She was confident the sample was good. According to the sample, the profile of the self-employed greatly resembled that of the Cuban labor force. That was a good sign. It is widely believed that the self-employed are younger, more educated and more predominantly women than the overall work force. However, the survey suggests otherwise. In fact, there was little difference in age, education, and gender between the sample and the general population of workers.

How Old Are They?

The age distribution of self-employed Cubans in the survey presents very few differences with the age distribution of the labor force. According to the *Anuario Estadístico de Cuba*, in 1989[5] the Cuban labor force was very young: 74.54 percent of Cubans who worked or were looking for a job were under forty-four years old. While only 0.03 percent are under 17 years old, and 15.6 percent are between seventeen and twenty-four years of age, 63.29 percent are between twenty-four and forty-four years old. The age distribution of the sample is very similar. Of those interviewed, 73.45 percent were under forty-four years old. None of the interviewees was younger than seventeen years old. Only minimal differences were found in more specific age brackets: 40.3 percent were between the ages of twenty-five and thirty-four (compared to

FIGURE 7.1   As Old as the Labor Force

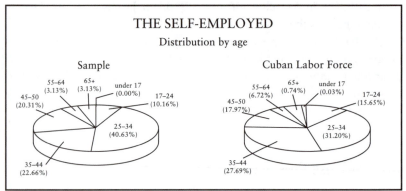

Source: Survey and Anuario Estadistico de Cuba, Comite de Estadica, Cuba 1989.

FIGURE 7.2   Similar Gender Profile

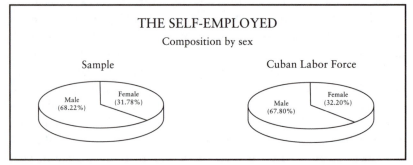

Source: Survey and Anuario Estadistico de Cuba, Comite Estatal de Estadicas, 1989.

31.20 percent in the general population) and 22.66 percent were between thirty-five and forty-four years old (compared to 27.69 percent
overall).

Thus, the survey provides evidence to suggest that the age profile of
the self-employed is very similar to that of the general population.

Does Gender Matter?

Not really. The gender profile of the sample is strikingly similar to
the labor force. While in the sample 31.78 percent of the interviewees
were female, women represent 32.80 percent of the total labor force.
The survey results also indicate that the proportion of men and women
vary according to the services. Males dominate certain forms of self-
employment: taxi drivers, booksellers, intermediaries for farm products,

FIGURE 7.3   **Similar Education Level**

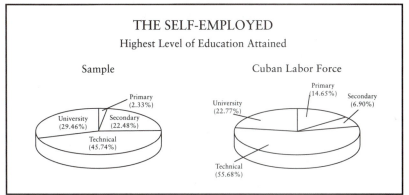

Source: Survey and Boletín Estadístico de Cuba, No. 5 January–May, Comité Statal de Estadistica, 1990.

and most technical services. Females dominate food services and artistry. In other words, gender matters only when analyzing specific activities.

How Educated Are They?

The level of education of those interviewed was very high; 75.2 percent have at least a technical school education. Only 2.33 percent

FIGURE 7.4   **Education Does Not Pay Off**

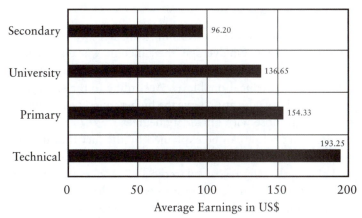

Source: Author survey.[6]

FIGURE 7.5   **Those Who Work More Make More**

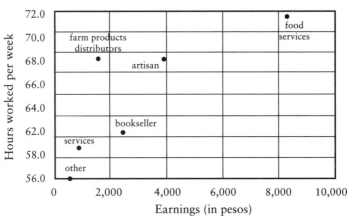

EARNINGS AND EDUCATION LEVEL

Source: Author survey.[6]

had not continued past primary school. The remaining 22.48 percent had a secondary school education. How do these levels compare to the Cuban labor force? According to the *Boletín Estadístico de Cuba* published in May 1990, similar figures apply to the total labor force in Cuba. The data reveals that 78.45 percent of Cubans who work or are looking for a job have at least a technical school education.

The next obvious question relates to the relationship between the level of education and the ability to earn a living as a self-employed.

Are the Most Educated Making More Money?

Everybody in the sample was earning considerably more than in their previous state jobs. On average, their income was eighteen times higher. Nevertheless, the survey shows there is no direct correlation between earnings and educational level. According to the survey, those with a technical school education have the highest average income: 41.4 percent more than those with university degrees.

This surprising result can be explained by the fact that university graduates are not free to offer services in their own professions. As mentioned above, they are restricted to the 157 services that have been liberalized by decree and hence cannot fully capitalize on their knowledge. Professors moonlighting as plumbers have a much smaller clientele than the real plumber.

FIGURE 7.6   **Those Who Earn More Buy in the Black Market**

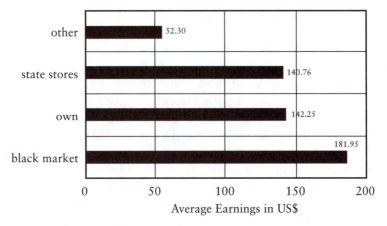

EARNINGS AND SOURCE OF MATERIALS

Source: Author survey.[6]

Freelancing in university professions is considered an act of corruption in Cuba. University graduates are expected to return to society what has been invested in their education. Medical doctors, professors, scientists, and engineers are considered the elite and their official salaries reflect that. They used to earn more than their less educated counterparts before joining the self-employed sector. The survey shows that in their previous jobs, university graduates earned 14.52 percent more than people with technical professions. This relation between income and educational level is different in the self-employment sector; those with technical education are making on average forty-one percent more than university graduates. Although differentials with regard to education disappear, all groups have experienced dramatic increases in their earnings.

Those Who Work More Earn More . . . But Wait, There's More

The survey shows that, on average, those interviewed worked sixty-five percent more in self-employment than in the state sector. They work an average sixty-six hours a week, with some working as much as 120 hours and others as little as thirty. There is a clear correlation between earnings and hours worked. Those engaged in food services are those who work the longest hours and earn the most: a little over 8,000 pesos, or US$400 per month.

Working longer hours does not seem to worry the self-employed. On the contrary, they usually express satisfaction over the freedom they feel: "I work as much as I want. If I want to make more money I work more. If I've had enough, I stop and go to the beach. Nobody can tell me what to do anymore. This is great."

While it is healthy that there is a correlation between earnings and effort, other factors influencing earnings in Cuba are signs of distortions. Since the private sector is not allowed to directly purchase its supplies in the market, only the government can legally sell raw materials to the self-employed. Nevertheless, there is a large black market for such material with a wider variety of better-quality, better-priced products than the legal market. The survey shows a correlation between earnings and the source of materials. A full seventy-one percent of interviewees named the black market as a source of inputs for their businesses. And the actual number is probably higher given the reluctance of respondents to admit their participation in the illegal black market.

The interviewees complained about the high prices and poor quality of supplies sold in state stores. Two shoe artisans argued that if they tried to sell sandals made with the poor quality plastic that the government calls leather, clients would call them thieves and insult them. "We don't have any other choice but to buy our supplies in the black market. If either the government or the consumer has to insult us, let it be the government. I care for my clients," says one of the interviewees. On the other hand, the government cares a lot about the earnings differentials and keeps raising taxes on everyone who buys or sells. Currently, this is the center of political tension in Cuba.

According to the survey, there is an important average earnings differential between those who buy their supplies in the black market and those who do so legally at state stores. The self-employed who do their shopping in the black market earn an average thirty percent more than their more legal counterparts.

Those Who Make More Money Pay More Taxes

The survey shows that in general those who earn more, also pay more taxes. Though the artisans, book sellers, distributors of farm products and other services show a clear correlation between earnings and taxes, food services seem to be paying proportionally less taxes. The opposite is true for tourism services, which are being overly taxed. Take taxis, for example, which are the most common tourism service: cars and bicycles are paying sixty-five percent—the highest tax noted in the sample even though their average earnings were among the lowest at below 2,000 pesos a month.

Recently, in July 1997, the government decided to create yet another tax for those negotiating with food. Every morning along the ocean waters facing the Havana seaside, dozens of fishermen sitting on big rubber tires try their luck fishing for their own consumption or for the black market. The government decided to tax this activity by charging them each a flat fee of US$15. "I now go fishing in the evening when they don't see me. I'm not paying US$15. What happens if I don't catch anything? I still have to pay, that's ridiculous! This is slavery!" a fisherman said.

Another tax imposed in 1997 has also outraged Cubans. Now, people who rent their rooms to tourists will also be visited by the taxman. According to some official estimates, twenty percent of the tourists visiting the island rent rooms in private houses instead of staying in hotels.

What Do the Self-employed Complain About?

Cubans are constantly complaining these days. They argue that life is hard, that prices are rising, and that the wider variety of things to buy in stores and markets is only available to those who can pay in dollars or its peso equivalent. Those who became self-employed have done so with the hope of a better life and of higher income. When asked, they mention the hope of having their own growing business. Nevertheless, a number of restrictions faced by the self-employed are making this goal unattainable: there are almost no markets for supplies, the self-employed have no access to credit, and they are prohibited from hiring workers outside their families. Everybody in Cuba violates this regulation. Jokingly Cubans argue that socialism has taught them that the whole country is a big family. Private property does not exist, so they can't buy space to expand on. Not even transportation equipment can be bought.

Despite this litany of restrictions, the one singled out as the most important impediment to the growth of their businesses was taxes; 51.94 percent pinpointed taxes as their biggest constraint. Lack of supplies was a distant second (19.39 percent) followed by lack of financing (16.28 percent) and the legal framework (2.33 percent).

Generally, the people interviewed felt harassed, disrespected, and exploited by the government. Cubans are expressing these sentiments of frustration and anger with great strength and conviction. Since they are no longer dependent on the government for their income, they have become more openly critical of the system. The government, in turn,

FIGURE 7.7   **Taxes Seem to Matter Most**

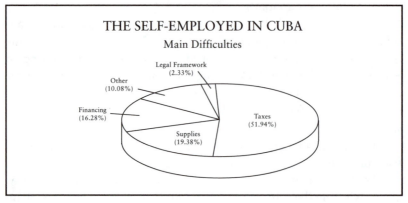

THE SELF-EMPLOYED IN CUBA
Main Difficulties

Legal Framework (2.33%)
Other (10.08%)
Financing (16.28%)
Taxes (51.94%)
Supplies (19.38%)

Source: Author Survey.[6]

has become aware of this political challenge. After three years of encouraging Cubans to join the sector, the leadership has begun to backtrack with ideological verbosity and outright harassment. This campaign has led many Cubans to believe that the self-employed are tainted with the characteristic selfishness of those who perform capitalist activities. Moreover, most Cubans tend to overestimate the earnings of the self-employed. Convinced that they are getting rich at the expense of someone else, traditional elites look down at them with a mixture of envy and resentment.

The small-scale entrepreneur in Cuba is trapped between socialism and capitalism, working wonders to make a profit despite the restrictions and distortions imposed by the socialist logic. These structural limitations—in frank contradiction with the entrepreneurial spirit—permeate the regulations for the private sector. Among other restrictions to eventual growth, the following are the most critical:

1. Lack of access to credit

2. Inability to hire workers outside the family

3. Absence of markets for supplies

4. Prohibited use of intermediaries

5. Very high income taxes

Many of these bottlenecks were supposed to be resolved by 1996. No major advances have been made and things have only worsened for the self-employed. Some analysts believe the government underestimated the political impact of a larger independent private sector and has now decided to impede its growth. Others look for answers in the huge distortions generated by the differential between the official and unofficial exchange rate. There are people in the private sector benefiting from the hidden subsidies in a variety of markets. Having been unable to unify the rates, the government is desperately trying to cope with the incentives to divert goods from one market to the other through taxes, administrative controls, and ideological speeches. Ironically, while the unification of the currency was delayed to avoid the negative social impact of inflation, the spillover effects of the distortions generated by the exchange differential are producing profound social discontent.

Making Shoes: What a Wonderful Feeling[6]

Jorge is a typical *cuentapropia*. At thirty-two years of age and with a technical background he fits in the general profile. Jorge used to work in a shoe factory and has been self-employed for the past two years. He likes what he is doing, but what he enjoys the most in his new job is the very private pleasure of the little freedom that comes with it. Jorge's working hours are long, but as he said: "It's my life, it's my decision, it's me. You probably can't understand what this means for me. For too many years we have been forced to hide ourselves, our personal needs and our freedom for the sake of others, in other words, for the success of the revolution."

Jorge likes to work at odd hours, he likes to raise the prices of his shoes, to lower them, to give them away to whomever he pleases, to speak out about and defend the need to develop the minuscule private sector open to Cubans. He is part of a new social breed who does not rely on the government to earn a decent living; and he is enjoying it with a vengeance.

He decided to take the risk, leave his job, and start his small business. Like many others he is

"I USED TO WORK FOR THE telephone company. I had to leave after the foreigners came to invest in the company. I am happy now. I live like a decent person: I eat three meals a day, I can dress in decent clothes, and I just bought a motorcycle. Well I paid a friend and he gave it to me. As a Cuban I can't legally own anything that the government has not assigned to me. So my friend has the papers and I have the moto.

"But there is too much envy. Since I have what I have, my neighbors have begun to ask questions. How did I get this, how did I get that. Envy, envy, and more envy is eating them up."

RAUL: *"THE OTHER DAY somebody told me that in La Sortija (a government supply store for the self-employed) they were finally selling some good leather. I went there and they had only Leather A, a horrible synthetic material. Believe me, the only way to do this is por debajo del tapete (cheating)."*

now legal. He got a license, but he had been selling his homemade shoes in the black market for the past ten years. It was an obvious business for him. He got the supplies by stealing them from the factory. He has a faithful clientele, who found in him the only source of shoes which fit properly. Before the recent market reforms, Cubans had two sources of goods: the *libreta* or rationing system, and the black market. Everything was rationed: food, shoes, and clothing. "The only problem was that if you didn't like the shoes, well, that was your problem and worse than that, if they didn't fit, that was *also* your problem." Many worked underground offering goods and services outside the controlled state system. Jorge added with pride, "The shoes are tailor-made for my clients."

How Much Money is Jorge Making?

About US$400 a month, almost twenty-five times more than his previous income. Everybody interviewed was earning considerably more than in their previous state jobs. On average, their income was eighteen times higher.

Where Does He Get His Supplies?

Cuba has no wholesale distributors. The Cuban government has not opened up the supply markets. Intermediaries are not only illegal, but unwanted. But probably one of the most important reasons to maintain tight control over the suppliers market is the huge differential between the official and unofficial exchange rates: one Cuban peso per U.S. dollar vs. 22 pesos per U.S. dollar. Although the difference has been dropping from 160 pesos per U.S. dollar in 1993, it is still a significant distortion that makes prices at least one twentieth of their real cost. The government's reluctance to unify has kept inflation under control but has also had a terrible impact on the economy. When Jorge is asked about where he has been buying the little equipment he uses to work, he answers coyly, "little by little I have been collecting it," but his smile seems to say, "Why are you asking such a dumb question?" And it is, in fact, a silly question. Everybody knows that there are no free markets for any of the instruments used by Jorge; nor are there supplies for most of the products the artisans make. They either take them from their workplaces (in other words steal them) or they buy them in the black market. Where do the products in the black market come from? From other workers who do the same thing. Everyone has to steal in Cuba for survival.

To the question: Where do you buy the leather, the thread, and the glue? "I buy those things at a market called *La Sortija*. There they sell me the leather, the soles, and the glue. I show them my license and they sell it to me." So that's where you bought the crocodile leather to make these sandals? The same smile . . . "But of course!" Then he shows a receipt from *La Sortija* for 80 pesos in leather products. He carries it with him to show the inspectors every time they come to harass and ask unpleasant questions. He has been using the same receipt for the past six months and it shows it: you can hardly see the numbers behind the wrinkled paper and the dirt. After a while he opens up more and says, "I usually buy all the material in the black market." The crocodile leather comes from *La Cienaga de Zapata* (Zapata Swamp). The other materials are from state enterprises. Jorge gets furious as he explains the awkward mechanism by which he gets his material. "Tell me something, you who live abroad, isn't this deceitful? The government allows us to make and sell shoes but doesn't give us the opportunity to buy the inputs. What does that mean? That we have to steal or induce others to do it. Why? Very simple: so they can get you if they want to, and send you to jail when they feel like it."

Cubans are constantly violating the laws. It's impossible not to for many, especially for those who are self-employed. Cubans usually are afraid of being caught doing something *illegal*: buying in the black market, charging excessive prices, having more than twelve chairs in a *paladar,* hiring non-relatives, lending money to others and charging interest rates, "buying" things like cars or motorcycles from other Cubans, selling shellfish in *paladares.* Many say that ultimately the greatest sin and worst illegality in Cuba is making money. After a while another artisan jumps into the conversation "Hey Jorgito, come on man," interrupts Luis, "if these *pinchos* (the slang word for anybody wearing a military uniform) want to get you, they don't need any of that

"CROCODILE SANDALS at 8 dollars?"

"Shhhhhh, lower your voice. It is prohibited to use crocodile leather. It comes from the Zapata Swamp. Hunting has been banned there for years."

bullshit you're talking about. The input markets? Come on! Since when do we need such sophisticated reasons? Or is it that you want to impress the foreigners with your opinion?" Luis is fifty years old, his skin is darkened by the sun, he takes out a plastic bottle with water and drinks from it, "I'm sure they've put us (the artisans) out here in the open so our brains fry up under the sun and we stop thinking."

The artisan's markets operate in empty urban areas, usually vacant lots left by collapsed buildings. The truth of the matter is that the government doesn't provide any assets (besides the empty space) for the self-employed to use. Luis has taken over the conversation now: "I can't stand to continue paying more taxes so those bureaucrats can sit in their air-conditioned offices while we don't even get a darn umbrella to stop the sun from drilling our skull! If I have to go to the bathroom during the eight hours that I have to spend here, I have to pay one peso to one of the nearby neighbors. I have to bring my table to put the shoes on, my chair to sit on, what is the government giving me for all the taxes we are paying?"

The interesting thing about this comment is that Cubans are, in fact, getting a lot from their government: free education and health, the rationing card, very low tariffs for public utilities, and above all a high indirect subsidy by keeping a huge foreign exchange differential.

How Does Jorge Set the Price?

A woman with a heavy Havana accent asks him for the price of the same pair of sandals a tourist is trying on. He doubts for a few seconds and decides to quote them both the same price: US$13. Usually in these markets, the artisans set higher prices for tourists than those offered to Cubans. The woman protests, visibly angry and frustrated since she can not afford them. She goes away criticizing the "abusive" prices and the profiteering of the *cuentapropias*. Jorge turns and says "these Cubans have become so unfriendly lately they only come to protest about the high prices. I know them very well." Cubans have, in fact, become much more aggressive with each other, especially with the self-employed.

How Many Hours Does Jorge Work?

Jorge comes to the market every day from 10 am to 5 or 6 pm, then he goes home to work where his wife and two daughters help him make shoes and sandals. "I work at night and sell during the day." That is the way he puts it when calculating the number of hours he devotes to his new job; twelve to fourteen hours a day, six days a week. Mondays are free to buy things and to do some errands. Jorge was working in a shoe factory, when the government decided to close it down. The workers were laid off with eighty percent of their average salary of the last five years. That meant 120 pesos (US$6) for him. "We can't live on that. Everything is very expensive these days." Cubans used to buy everything through the rationing system; not anymore.

Working longer hours doesn't seem to worry the self-employed. Quite the opposite. They're usually happy to be free to do as they please. For Jorge now the choice of whether to work or not is dictated by his needs and desires and not the government. For that he is thankful.

Total Satisfaction or Your Money Back

Cubans prefer to buy from the self-employed than from the state. To buy in a state store means little choice, poor service, and no possibility of returning bad merchandise. The self-employed sector has introduced competition, not only among themselves, but with the government sector as well. "What the government hates is that people are choosing more to buy from us than from their stores. You can't blame the consumer. We give them better prices, better quality, and a complete guarantee: if something is wrong with the product, we fix it or give the money back."

Politics Is in the Air

"I am an economist, I work at the ministry of basic industries, I listen quite often to Radio Martí. Cubans in Miami are very superficial in their analysis of the situation here. Since I was born—and I am twenty-four years old—I have been taught to see the good and the bad side of things. I am sick and tired of this political system in which you can only choose from a group of one. But those guys in Miami they don't have a clue of what is happening here. They have never come here and they keep telling us that we should get organized and revolt. How? Besides, the more they say the more difficult it is to get organized. They should come here to realize how ridiculous that sounds here. Let the Americans come and make a secret poll. I bet the result would be that the majority of Cubans want freedom but they want the Cubans on the island to do the changing, not them."

Legal, But Not Legitimate

The Cuban government has been opening up the economy in order to increase the efficiency of state enterprises. While the country is thriving on state capitalism, private entrepreneurs have been legalized, but not legitimized. They are regarded as a transitory, necessary evil. Nevertheless, according to many analysts, the liberalization of the self-employed sector has been one of the most important reforms in Cuba. These small Cuban entrepreneurs are facing unique restraints and opportunities within a complex set of regulations.

When compared with the general labor force, they show striking similarities in age, education, and gender. Interestingly, there is no correlation between earnings and educational level. In state jobs, university graduates had the highest income. In the self-employment sector, everybody is better off, but those with a technical education are the most successful.

There was an explosion of newcomers to the sector in 1995, but there has been a decline over the past two years. Many suggested they would go underground if the government kept increasing red tape and income taxes.

Earnings are not only a function of effort, although clearly those who work more, earn more. There is also evidence that those who buy their materials in the black market earn more than those who buy them in state stores. In other words, earnings are also correlated with the many distortions generated by the huge differential between the official and unofficial exchange rates.

In order to recuperate the rent appropriated by the self-employed by virtue of these distortions, the government has been raising taxes constantly since 1995 and created a politically explosive situation. Cubans are angry. In the survey, most of them identified taxes as the single most important problem for the development of their businesses. This is particularly interesting when compared with the other major restrictions faced by the self-employed. As it turns out, the inaccessibility of capital, supplies, or distributors doesn't seem to bother them as much as taxes do.

When in 1993, the Cuban government began to open up the economy and to implement market-oriented reforms, the legalization of dollars and the liberalization

"HOW MUCH ARE you paying in taxes now?"

"I am paying in taxes the equivalent of the salaries of ten government employees. That is more than enough. What else do they want?"

of professions were the most important reforms oriented to benefit the average Cuban. Four years later, the self-employment sector, after reaching its peak in 1995, has shrunk, while those who are still in it, are tired of government harassment.

While the self-employed worry about taxes, the government worries about the earnings generated by foreign exchange distortions. This game has tremendous political implications, which are difficult to predict. Ironically, the government has not unified the exchange rate to avoid the negative political and social impact of inflation. The delay in unifying has had political consequences anyway, and put the legitimacy of the self-employed in the balance.

Understanding Salaries in Cuba

Salaries in Cuba are low. In 1997, the average salary was 160 pesos per month. Salaries in dollars are usually calculated by dividing the peso income by the unofficial exchange rate. According to this calculation the average dollar salary in 1997 was close to US$7 per month. Along these same lines, all salaries in the public sector are very low if calculated in dollars. A secretary makes 200 pesos or US$9, a university professor makes 450 pesos or US$20, a vice-minister 400 pesos, and a minister 500 pesos or US$22. These calculations infuriate government officials in Cuba. "When you say outside (of Cuba) that the salary is US$7, people think that we are a bunch of slaves who work for nothing. They forget that the rationing card is sold at a small fraction of its value. They forget about free education and health. They do not understand what socialism is all about."

On the other hand most Cubans complain about the rationing card and how the number of items available has been shrinking constantly since 1989. According to the people interviewed, the list of things they used to buy with the rationing card was as follows: kerosene, meat, chicken, eggs, rice, beans, vegetables, marmalade, tomato paste, salt, sugar, cooking oil, cereal, flour, crackers, coffee, milk, pasta, matches, cigarettes, sodas, rum, soap, toothpaste, tampons, and detergent. Nowadays, the food they can get with the rationing card or libreta, is less. By July 1997, six pounds of rice per person per month was available, also three pounds of unrefined and another three pounds of refined sugar. Seven eggs per person, one piece of bread per day per person, a liter of milk for children under seven years of age per day, a liter of soy yogurt for children between seven and thirteen years old. A tube of toothpaste per person and a bar of soap per family per month. Four ounces of coffee and a quarter pound of salt. Sometimes beans or potatoes. Four ounces of coffee are usually available. Every three of four months a quarter liter of oil arrives and twice a year a small amount of fish or meat is available. Women get tampons twice a year and on mother's day everyone gets a cake. Prices for the rationing card are a small fraction relative to the dollar stores. The difference in price on average reflects the foreign exchange differential. In other words, if the exchange rate is 20 pesos per dollar, prices in the dollar stores are approximately twenty times higher than those found in the rationing card.

In order to make a more accurate estimate of the average salary for Cubans, the calculation must take into consideration the huge hidden subsidies in the controlled peso economy. In fact, it is not fair to compare salaries by dividing the average income of the family by the unofficial exchange rate. According to different sources and to the budgets shown below, a Cuban family of four spends about 160 pesos in the controlled subsidized economy. The food from the rationing card, public transportation, utilities, and housing are priced at the official exchange rate of one peso per US dollar. Therefore, on average, the first 160 pesos earned by Cubans give them a purchasing power of 160 dollars. Those pesos earned above 160 can buy very little more at subsidized prices. Almost all goods will have to be bought at dollar stores or at liberalized peso markets where competitive prices reflect the unofficial exchange rate of 22 pesos per U.S. dollar. In other words, the formula to calculate the real salary would be:

$$\text{Real Salary} = 160 + (W-160)/UE$$

Where W is the salary and UE the unofficial exchange rate.

The unofficial exchange rate in July 1997 was 22 pesos per U.S. dollar. According to this formula, a family of four, with both parents making 500 pesos each as university professors, has an income equivalent to US\$169. This figure is considerably higher than the US$45 which results from dividing 1,000 pesos by the unofficial exchange rate.

Monthly Budget for Two Families of Four in 1997

	University professors	Self-employed
Income per month	1,000 pesos	8,602 pesos
Expenses:		
* Rationing card	70 pesos	70 pesos
* Utilities	27 pesos	39 pesos
* Rent	30 pesos	11 pesos
* Transportation	40 pesos	29 pesos
Total expenses in the controlled economy	167 pesos	149 pesos

What the libreta does not provide must be bought at the farmers' market, dollar stores, or in the black market. Families who earn in dollars tend to spend less in the black market and more in dollar stores.

Notes

1. Ronald Reagan, *An American Life* (New York: Simon and Schuster, 1990).
2. Private restaurants usually operating in the living room and dining room of private homes. These restaurants have been so successful that in 1997 the government introduced a similar concept of small places to eat run by the state.
3. Debate over the legalization of self-employed workers. The National Assembly, December 28, 1993.
4. Reuters World Service, April 24, 1996.
5. Unfortunately there is no more recent published information.
6. The survey was conducted in Havana during March and April 1997. Two-hundred thirty-four self-employed people were interviewed in four farmer's markets, three major artisan's markets, and *paladares*. Taxi drivers (in cars and bicycles) and a variety of independently run self-employed businesses were also interviewed. The sample was selected at random and includes people with diverse activities and from different sectors of Havana and Pinar del Rio. Only 218 questionnaires were processed because of errors in the data collected. Although this is a small sample for the purpose of strong statistical inferences, it paints a relatively clear picture in some areas.

8

BIGGER-IS-BETTER CAPITALISM

> When you don't know where you are going, it does
> not matter which way you go.
>   Cheshire Cat, *Alice in Wonderland*
>   Lewis Carroll[1]

While the small Cuban entrepreneur is fighting for economic survival and social recognition, foreign investors in Cuba are enjoying the red carpet treatment. Donning the secrets of success for Cuba's economic restructuring—technology, capital, markets, and managerial skills—investors from over twenty-five countries are the new partners of Cuba's socialist government. Political speeches and management memos are now peppered with buzzwords like *competitiveness, efficiency, profit centers, marketing* and *customer satisfaction*. In other words, while the traditional elites consider private capitalism a short-term necessary evil, the government is thriving on state capitalism. As Finance Minister José Luis Rodriguez pointed out in 1997:

> The economic program has two objectives: first, we have to resist the impact of the crisis and second, Cuba must re-enter the world economy. It must become competitive and penetrate international markets. External trade must be changed and to do that we need foreign investment, that is our instrument.[2]

The international press views legalized dollar trading and self-employment as evidence that Cuba is moving toward a free-market economy. The self-employed are now ubiquitous on the island, and the stories of scrappy entrepreneurs eking out a living in a socialist system are fascinating. To the casual observer, these trends may seem to herald the arrival of capitalism to the Cuban economy and society. However, there's something missing. In Cuba, private capitalism has not been ideologically accepted yet. Despised by the traditional elite, the self-employed have been *legalized,* but not *legitimized* by the establishment. Instead of future capitalists, they are the land rafters of the socialist economy. Like those who have left the system by sea, the land rafters are left on their own to accomplish an almost impossible task.

Various government officials and party leaders have voiced their disdain for the self-employed. "We do not want petty capitalism here, we are not going to copy capitalism from the poor." They are referring to the growing informal sector in other Latin American countries.

But state capitalism is different. Less visible and less well-known, it is bringing a fundamental change to the Cuban economic system. State capitalism has emerged in Cuba, and its development is key to the survival of the Cuban revolution. Unlike the other economic reforms of the 1990s such as self-employment and the legalization of dollar holdings, government joint ventures with foreign investors have been embraced by the regime. While private capitalism remains stigmatized, state capitalism has been both legalized and legitimized. For Cuban policymakers, when it comes to capitalism, bigger is better.

The evolution of state capitalism has had two major components:

- Decentralization to improve the efficiency of previously centrally managed state companies, and

- Foreign investment in joint ventures with the government.

Efficiency, Instead of Subsidies

With subsidies to state enterprises down from 5.4 billion pesos in 1993 to 1.4 billion pesos in 1996, managers are now concerned more about profit margins than production quotas. This dramatic belt-tightening, combined with foreign competition, has altered the incentive structure for both managers and workers in Cuban enterprises. As foreign investment flows into Cuba in the form of joint ventures, Cuban industry has become even more decentralized as it is forced to acquire the discipline of the market. In 1993, the government published a list of 132 enterprises in all sectors—with the exception of health and defense—that had been targeted for joint ventures. Decentralization helps streamline companies and make them more attractive to foreign investors; when foreign investment arrives, it stimulates further decentralization. When one company in an industry enters into a joint venture with a foreign company, other companies are forced to compete with the joint venture, streamline their production processes and become more efficient. "Tell me what you need for your conference. Let me prove to you that this hotel can provide you better service, better food, and better logistical support than any competitor," said a young Cuban general manager of a hotel in Havana. For many ex-Marxists, becoming a manager in a joint venture company has become an attractive career opportunity.

Decentralization does not polarize Cuban officials the way other market reforms do. Instead, it represents a way for the regime to improve efficiency without dismantling socialism in an obvious manner. The transition of state enterprises from centrally planned, quota-oriented entities with soft budget constraints to profit centers is one of the fundamental changes underway in the Cuban economy. Since it is less controversial, decentralization may prove to be the most significant change since 1989.

Decentralization has been most prevalent in the foreign trade sector. Any company that produces exportable goods may be granted authorization to export directly: "Given the severe economic contraction we experienced, it was necessary to put an end to the state monopoly and decentralize trade. Today, around 281 companies perform external trade operations with over 3,000 companies in 132 countries."[3]

Exporting companies are also responsible for their own financing; export receipts are to be used to purchase imported inputs such as oil and other raw materials. Financial autonomy is a priority, but these firms can continue to receive some support from the central government in order to purchase machinery and equipment. The Ministry of Foreign Trade assists and supports exporting firms' attempts to penetrate foreign markets, and approves direct exporting on a case-by-case basis.[4]

Companies that had previously been confined to research and development, particularly in the pharmaceutical and health care industries, are now responsible for producing and selling their products abroad. Many firms have altered their organizational structure to be able to respond to market forces more quickly. Marketing teams have been created and trained in international management techniques. They have begun producing analyses of markets and competitors' positions. Further, Cuban firms in some industries are hiring foreign sales forces in the market they seek to enter. At the University of Havana, the first MBA class graduated in February 1997, having completed courses ranging from accounting to foreign trade. The government has instituted a system of bonuses as well. Paid in cash or in kind, some 1.3 million Cuban workers have received bonuses.[5]

Law-Decree 147 of 1994 charged the State Central Administration Organization (AOCE, Organismo de la Administracion Central del Estado) with directing structural changes in the Cuban state to "create progressively the conditions for the decentralized functioning of the state business sector."[6] Law-Decree 147 streamlined the Cuban bureaucracy to limit ministries to policy-making roles while granting more decision-making power to businesses. The law makes businesses responsible for the administration of equipment and financial resources, allowing them to grow to an optimal size and operate with greater flexibility and independence.

The Kaloney Case

The Cuban shoe manufacturer Kaloney is a good example of the changes Cuban industries have effected in recent years. In the 1980s, it was a large, inflexible conglomerate whose production plans were based on meeting centrally mandated targets. In 1990, however, Kaloney was divided into nine plants that produced differentiated products. The plants were given control over their production processes, and a just-in-time manufacturing system was installed, while a holding company was established to oversee the company's finances. Decentralization helped Kaloney achieve significant productivity gains: the cycle of production was reduced from thirteen days to just two days, production was diversified, and the defect rate fell substantially. Meanwhile, a bonus system was implemented allowing workers to earn bonuses of up to forty percent of their salaries if production, quality, and efficiency targets were met.

The Odd Couple

Foreign investors have brought more than just hard currency to the island. The government has found a new partner to help restructure Cuban industry. Foreign managers have played an important role in changing the mentality of government officials, introducing market-oriented incentives that have been essential to Cuba's survival. Nevertheless, there is an important question that remains unanswered: How long can these companies survive with high government intervention? The lesson from other countries, especially in Latin America, is that there are inherent limits to the ability of state capitalism to improve efficiency and competitiveness; state-led industrialization has been abandoned throughout the region in favor of an aggressive process of privatization. Nevertheless, the restructuring of the Cuban economy is a fundamental change that has enabled the country to weather the economic and political storms of the 1990s, and its importance should not be underestimated.

Foreign investment in automobiles fuels the ire of those who must make do with their revolutionary relics.

Doing Business with the Government? Good Luck!

Antonio Rodríguez was very excited. He had been waiting for a long time to do business with Cuba. Now that foreign investment was being welcomed, he had a concrete offer to make. After more than twenty years working in the optical business, he knew all about cost structures and markets for different types of optical frames. Cuba could be a great market for plastic injection technology; it's low cost, simple, and efficient. He had the machinery, money, and know-how.

After various meetings in Havana, he finally scheduled a meeting with the *compañero* in charge of that area. "He is going to answer all your questions and of course, we are very interested. We have an important deficit of eyeglasses. They are too expensive for most people," said somebody from the Foreign Investment Ministry.

Antonio was confident. If the problem was high cost, he had the answer. He was going to pull off this deal. After making a thorough presentation, he was handed a quick, but rather rude, response.

"We are sorry, Mr. Rodríguez," the bureaucrat answered, "you don't seem to understand, there is not enough demand for eyeglasses right now. You see, the installed capacity we already have in the country greatly exceeds demand. We don't need any more frame manufacturers."

"But, let me explain, what *I* understand is that you're having a problem reducing costs. Your demand is probably low because your prices are too high. I can bring new technology to reduce costs and offer cheaper products for those who can't pay the higher prices currently being offered. Demand will increase."

"Mr. Rodríguez," answered the *compañero* in charge of that area as he stood up, "it has been a pleasure meeting you, but we're not interested."

With that answer, Antonio returned to Colombia thinking, "these guys are full of it. They are just like any other bureaucrat in Latin America managing a state-owned enterprise. They don't care about the business. They only care about preserving their little quota of power. They're afraid of the competition. And they should be. I'm not coming back."

But Many Are Coming Back

In spite of many disappointing stories like Antonio's, the Cuban government is associating more and more with foreign companies in a variety of economic sectors. Law-Decree 77, passed in 1995, officially opened up to foreign investment all sectors of the Cuban economy except education, public health, and the armed forces. This is an important provision because under the previous law, the government had to determine whether each sector of proposed investment was suitable for such investment. Law-Decree 77 replaces the 1982 Law-Decree 50 and reverses many of the deficiencies of that law, which prohibited investment in most sectors of the economy.

The rationale for expanding the field for associations is presented in the law:

> Such investment can usher in the introduction of innovative and advanced technology, the modernization of industries, greater efficiency in production, the creation of new jobs, improvement in the quality of the products and services it offers, cost reduction, greater competitiveness abroad, and access to certain markets, which as a whole would boost the efforts of the country in its economic and social development.[7]

Law-Decree 77 stipulates three forms of foreign investment: joint ventures, economic association contracts, and corporations of one hundred percent foreign ownership. Joint ventures establish a new legal entity separate from any of the parties to the venture. The foreign and Cuban investors must negotiate their respective capital contributions, which take the form of nominative shares. A public document must detail the bylaws, including the management structure and decision-making mechanisms. A joint venture is established when these documents are entered into the Registry of Republic of Cuba's Chamber of Commerce. A contract of economic association, which does not create a separate legal entity but is a business partnership, is the second mode of foreign investment under the new law. These too are legally established once the contract is presented to the Chamber of Commerce Registry. The third mode of foreign investment is the totally foreign capital company, in which the foreign investor, acting as an individual or as a corporation, is the sole owner and manager of a company.

Law-Decree 77 also permits foreign investment in real estate for the first time in socialist Cuba. Foreign investors can build or buy housing and tourism facilities for private residents who are "not permanent residents in Cuba." They are permitted to invest in housing or offices for foreign companies, as well as in "real estate development for use in tourism."[8]

The statute requires foreign investors to employ Cuban nationals according to existing labor and social security legislation. There has been no change in the procurement of Cuban labor; workers must still be provided by an employing entity contracted by the Ministry of Foreign Investment and Economic Cooperation, although individual investors have received some concessions in this area.[9] This employing entity receives the workers' salaries in dollars, then pays them in pesos at the official rate of one dollar to the peso. For example, if in 1998—when the un-official exchange rate was approximately 20 pesos per dollar—a waiter got paid US$400 a month, the government agency would keep the 400 dollars and pay the waiter 400 Cuban pesos, calculating the exchange at the official rate of one Cuban peso per dollar instead of twenty per dollar. Top administrative and technical posts may be filled by foreigners. If the investor chooses to fill top spots with Cubans, he may hire them directly.[10] If a foreign investor wants to fire a Cuban employee, the employing entity may replace the worker with another, and pay indemnity to the dismissed employee.

According to various sources, as of 1997 there were around three hundred foreign investment agreements with over twenty-five countries. The Cuban government announced in February 1998 that foreign companies had invested in 332 joint ventures; 317 by the end of 1997 and an additional fifteen had been approved during the first two months of 1998.[11] According to the same government sources, seventy-five percent of the investments are concentrated in tourism, construction,

TABLE 8.1 Foreign Investment in Cuba as of Oct. 17, 1998. U.S. Dollars

Country	Announced	Delivered
Total	6,119,000,000	1,766,900,000
Australia	500,000,000	n.a.
Austria	500,000	100,000
Brazil	150,000,000	20,000,000
Canada	1,807,000,000	600,000,000
Chile	69,000,000	30,000,000
China	10,000,000	5,000,000
Dominican Republic	5,000,000	1,000,000
France	100,000,000	50,000,000
Germany	10,000,000	2,000,000
Greece	2,000,000	500,000
Honduras	7,000,000	1,000,000
Israel	22,000,000	7,000,000
Italy	397,000,000	387,000,000
Jamaice	2,000,000	1,000,000
Japan	2,000,000	500,000
Mexico	1,806,000,000	450,000,000
The Netherlands	300,000,000	40,000,000
Panama	2,000,000	500,000
Portugal	15,000,000	10,000,000
Russia	25,000,000	2,000,000
South Africa	400,000,000	5,000,000
Spain	350,000,000	100,000,000
Sweden	10,000,000	1,000,000
United Kingdom	75,000,000	50,000,000
Uraguay	300,000	300,000
Venezuela	50,000,000	3,000,000

Source: U.S.-Cuba Trade and Economic Council, Inc.

agriculture, food, and light industry. Foreign investment activities accounted for twenty percent of Cuba's Gross National Product by the beginning of 1998.[12]

However, the numbers related to announced investments versus those delivered vary significantly. The Cuban government stated that over US$2.1 billion had been committed by 1996. According to the U.S.-Cuba Trade and Economic Council, in July 1996 over US$5 billion had been announced and less than US$800 million delivered. According to The Economist Intelligence Unit, US$620 million were expected in 1998. These figures have become increasingly sensitive due to the mounting tension between Cuba and the United States. In spite of the restrictions imposed by the U.S. government, reports are that about 1,500 representatives of American firms have made "fact-finding" trips to the island, often at the invitation of the Cuban government.[13]

Despite the withdrawal of Grupo Domos's telecom venture, Mexico remains the largest investor in Cuba. According to different sources, companies based there have committed or delivered US$450 million, with other deals announced but not yet completed totaling US$1.4 billion. Mexican investments are concentrated in tourism, transportation, petroleum, consumer goods, and manufacturing. Italy is the second biggest investor, with US$387 million currently invested and an additional US$1.2 billion planned. The Italians have focused on textiles, tourism, telecommunications, and Fiat automobiles. Canada is a distant third, with US$150 million currently invested and an additional US$1.2 billion planned. There are over a dozen Canadian mining firms in Cuba; other Canadian investors have gone into finance, petroleum, tourism, communications, brewing, and tobacco. Fourth place belongs to Spain which has invested US$120 million and plans to invest US$350 million more. Spanish investors are primarily involved in tourism, energy, manufacturing, and tobacco. British firms have invested US$50 million mostly in pharmaceuticals and chemicals.

It is difficult to determine how much money foreign investors have pumped into Cuba. Nevertheless, government officials in 1997 insisted that over US$2.1 billion and three hundred associations[14] had been committed. These are probably ballpark figures and good enough to illustrate a trend.[15]

For many companies, beating the U.S. business sector to Cuba is part of the attraction. Most joint ventures are in either tourism or export-oriented products. Tourism has flourished thanks to important Spanish investments. Citrus exports have been boosted thanks to investment from Israel, Greece, and Chile. Nickel and mining has attracted Canadian companies.

TABLE 8.2   Countries with Whom Cuba Has Signed
Protection Agreements: Dates of the Agreements

Italy	7/5/93
Russia	7/7/93
Spain	25/5/94
Colombia	6/7/94
U.K.	20/1/95
China	20/4/95
Bolivia	6/5/95
Ukraine	20/5/95
Vietnam	12/10/95
Lebanon	12/10/95
Argentina	30/11/95
South Africa	8/12/95
Chile	10/1/96
Rumania	27/1/96
Barbados	12/2/96
Germany	30/4/96
Greece	8/6/96
Switzerland	28/6/96

Source: El Comercio Exterior y la Inversion Extranjera en la
Economía Cubana en 1996. By Perez Omar. In La Economía
Cubana en 1966: Resultados, Problemas y Perspectivas. Centro
de Estudios de la Economía Cubana. (CEE), La Habana, 1997.

Recently, many new joint ventures have been formed to sell to the
domestic market in Cuba. As a result, tourism firms have become less
dependent on imports for such inputs as towels, sheets, furniture, stoves,
air conditioners, food and beverage products, and construction materials. Joint ventures in tourism and other sectors are stimulating the
formation of other joint ventures to supply them at a low cost. This
process of integration will increase in the future, and provide an important dynamic to the Cuban economy, helping the country improve its
trade balance. The increase in joint ventures does not seem to have

Not everything is old and crumbling in Havana (Mercado de Carlos III).

slowed significantly as a result of the tightening of the U.S. embargo in 1996 with the enactment of the Helms-Burton Law as we will see in the next chapter. Nevertheless it has scared away some small investors who find any potential U.S. threat too costly to risk.

To aid it in its search for partners, Cuba has made an effort to strike investment protection and promotion agreements with foreign governments. These agreements have promoted a more favorable investment climate for companies of the signatory countries. These government-to-government agreements are also a way for Cuba to recruit allies to face down expropriation claims by the U.S. government or Cuban-Americans. As of 1994, agreements had been signed with a large number of governments. The agreements vary between countries, but they are all structurally similar. They provide protection against nationalization and expropriation, except for reasons of public or national interest, and in other exceptional cases. The host country must compensate the nationalized firm at a fair market value in a convertible currency. The agreements guarantee equal treatment and the repatriation of investment and they establish a dispute resolution mechanism. They also provide for compensation for losses in the event of war or other states of emergency.[16] Clearly, these agreements are indicative of Cuba's genuine effort to create a stable and attractive investment climate.

In some ways, promoting foreign investment is a balancing act for the Cuban government. On the one hand, it recognizes the need to grant foreign investors the means to motivate their workers. On the other hand, it wants to minimize income inequality. For this reason, the law allows for the creation of an economic stimulus fund, but stipulates that the government regulate the size of the contributions to these funds. These incentives are typically paid in dollars and can represent a significant portion of a worker's pay.

The new law provides certain guarantees to foreign investors, stating they shall "enjoy full protection and security and their assets cannot be expropriated." The law sets forth exceptions, however, for reasons of "the public good or in the interest of society"—terms that are not explicitly defined. In the case of expropriation, the Cuban government will provide compensation in a freely convertible currency, the value of which would be determined via negotiations between the foreign investor and the government. If they are unable to arrive at a mutually agreeable compensation, "an organization with internationally recognized prestige" would act as an arbiter.[17]

Those who consider self-employment the barometer of Cuba's economic reform climate may be using the wrong measurement. Harassment of the small entrepreneur does not imply a rejection of capitalism alltogether. In fact, the opened-arms approach to foreign investment suggests quite the opposite.

Why the difference? Actually, it's easy to see why, when faced with a choice, the Cuban government prefers large foreign investments over which it has some measure of control to small individual investors over whom it has virtually no control at all. There is some space in Cuba's ideology for joint ventures with foreign capital, while individual profit seekers are ideologically anathema. Foreign investors can be viewed as contributors to the overall economic pie. The self-employed are seen as slicing off slivers of that pie, defying the government's distributive powers and challenging the principle of equality.

For now, foreign investment is the preferred form of capitalism for Cuban officials, who have toned down their socialist rhetoric to make overtures to entrepreneurs overseas. The Cuban regime is thriving on state capitalism, and an increasing number of foreign companies are accepting the risks of joining a partnership with these once committed revolutionaries.

Notes

1. Lewis Carroll. *Alice in Wonderland* (New York: Scholastic Paperbacks, 1988).
2. José Luis Rodríguez, finance minister, conference in Havana, April 1997.
3. José Luis Rodríguez, La Economia Cubana. Situacion en 1997 y Perspectivas, ECLAC conference, October 1997.
4. Collins, "Cuba: Crisis and the Road to Recovery," in Heath, ed., *Revitalizing Socialist Enterprise.*
5. DeGeorge, "A Touch of Capitalism."
6. "Cuba's Economy During the Special Period in Peacetime: Changes and Transformations." Article broadcast by Cuban economist Silvia Domenech Nieves for Prensa Latina news agency, Havana, March 29, 1995.
7. Cuban Foreign Investment Act (CFIA), second introductory paragraph.
8. CFIA, Article 16.1.
9. Interview with Grupo Domos President Garza Calderon. Article 35 of the CFIA states that "special labor regulations" can be established in "exceptional cases."
10. CFIA, Article 31.1.
11. Agence France Presse, February 1998.
12. Cuban foreign investment minister, Ibrahim Ferradaz.
13. Cuba Survey, *The Economist,* 15
14. José Luis Rodríguez, ECLAC Conference, Mexico City, October 1997.
15. CEPAL, 1997.
16. *Columbia Journal of World Business,* March 22, 1995.
17. CFIA, Article 3.

9

WHAT COMES NEXT? ENDING THE LONG-DISTANCE CIVIL WAR

> War is a continuation of policy by other means. It is not merely a political act but a real political instrument.
>
> Karl von Clausewitz
> *War, Politics and Power*[1]

> There is no working middle course in wartime.
>
> Sir Winston Churchill[2]

A beautiful Caribbean island, strategically located, with superb beaches, fertile land, and a well-educated population—in short, a country with tremendous potential for growth and development. What prevents Cuba from harnessing its potential? Will it ever be able to do so? Will it eventually join its neighbors throughout the hemisphere and adopt a system of civil, political, and economic liberties?

Some blame Cuba's appallingly low income on the inherent inefficiencies of the communist system. Socialist economic incentives end up conspiring against productivity and efficiency. Without a decentralized decision-making process by market-oriented firms underpinned by a property system that allows resources to be mobilized, it is impossible to exploit the opportunities that propel growth. But critics argue that China has been able to grow rapidly and in a sustained manner in spite of its Communist political regime. Why can't Cuba do the same?

Others blame it all on Fidel Castro. According to this Castro-centric analysis, if he were out of the picture, Cuba would quickly return to the fold and adopt civil, political, and economic liberties that would allow individuals to work for their own benefit and thus develop the country. This view assumes there is no real constituency behind Fidel and that the restrictions on freedom are the product of his devious personal machinations.

Others still blame it all on the embargo. Were it not for the restrictions on Cuba's access to its natural markets, its resources would be better utilized, its people would be more engaged in commercial activities, and market incentives would transform society.

Each of these explanations may provide a piece of the puzzle, but in a fundamental sense they miss the big picture. The missing piece that makes the Cuban puzzle make sense is the long-distance civil war still raging between those who won in 1959 and those who lost out. Understanding the nature of that confrontation, its participants, and the weapons involved helps explain its effects and imagine its resolution.

What War?

What is meant by a decades-old long-distance civil war? After all, didn't the Cuban revolution triumph in 1959? Hasn't it kept a tight control over domestic affairs? In what sense can we talk about a civil war?

Obviously, the reference to distance alludes to the confrontation between the government in Cuba and a segment of the exile community in the United States. But didn't that community lose all it had? How can they still be an important force shaping Cuba's destiny?

The early years of the revolution put an end to a hot, local civil war, but ushered in a more distant, colder confrontation between those who left their assets and social positions and those who took them over. Each side in this confrontation joined forces with one of the two superpowers then engaged in the Cold War, and the Cuban issue became an East-West fault line. The winners took over agricultural land, real estate, and productive assets. The losers joined forces with the United States and attempted military action before settling on the trade embargo as the weapon of choice.

Those who took over in Cuba needed a political system that would prevent the losers, armed with the international support of an awesome player, from regaining power. Their weapon of choice was the adoption of a regime that prevented the exiles (and many others) from taking back their property or their political power.

Each side knew their weapons were hurting innocent bystanders. Trade sanctions hurt everyone on the island, not just those in power. They even made life more difficult for those exiles with family ties, restricting their ability to visit relatives and at times even making it illegal to help their families out.

Restrictions on civil and political rights by the power structure in Havana constrained the political ambitions of those wanting to overthrow the regime, but also prevented those who stayed from expressing their views, developing new ideas, and shaping the course of their destiny.

Weapon of Choice: The External Embargo

Early in the revolution, U.S. corporate interests and geo-political concerns took precedence over the civil confrontation. In the early years, the exile community was too weak to have much impact on the U.S. political process, but over time, its influence has expanded dramatically. On the one hand, corporations have long written off their lost Cuban assets. On the other, the Cold War is over, radically changing the geo-political game. By the time the Soviet Union collapsed, the Cuban exile community had adopted U.S. citizenship and had learned how to play the domestic political game. This community pressured for a series of congressional actions that wrested control of Cuban policy away from the executive administration and into the hands of its own lobby. In this light, the Torricelli Act of 1992 and the Helms-Burton Act of 1996 can best be interpreted as the final attempts to overthrow the Cuban Revolution by tightening the embargo just when the Cuban government had been weakened by the Soviet collapse.

The Torricelli Act prohibited U.S. subsidiaries from trading with Cuba and restricted ships that traded with Cuba from docking in the United States. Its goals were to prevent U.S. companies and foreign partners from circumventing the embargo through foreign operations.

The Helms-Burton Act is far more than this. It is a thirty-nine–page law consisting of four titles. Title I seeks additional sanctions against the Cuban government. It includes a laundry list of new ways for the United States to pressure the Cuban regime. For example, it directs the Secretary of the Treasury to instruct U.S. directors of international financial institutions like the World Bank or the Inter-American Development Bank to oppose the admission of Cuba into those organizations. It also makes any independent state of the former Soviet Union that provides assistance or engages in "non-market"-based trade with Cuba ineligible for U.S. assistance.

Title II requires the President of the United States to develop an assistance plan for a transitional or elected government in Cuba. The law goes into extensive detail about what the United States would accept as a transitional government. To begin with, both Fidel and Raul Castro are prohibited from participating in such a government. Secondly, the government must make clear commitments to return the properties taken over since 1959 to current U.S. citizens, including those who were Cuban citizens when their properties were expropriated. Hence, transition means winning the civil war.

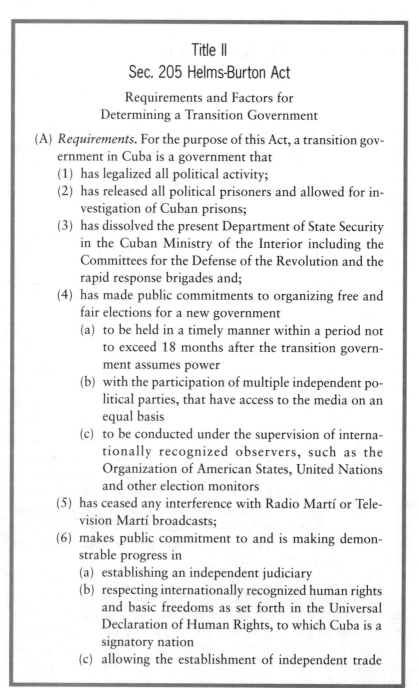

Title II
Sec. 205 Helms-Burton Act

Requirements and Factors for
Determining a Transition Government

(A) *Requirements.* For the purpose of this Act, a transition government in Cuba is a government that

(1) has legalized all political activity;

(2) has released all political prisoners and allowed for investigation of Cuban prisons;

(3) has dissolved the present Department of State Security in the Cuban Ministry of the Interior including the Committees for the Defense of the Revolution and the rapid response brigades and;

(4) has made public commitments to organizing free and fair elections for a new government

   (a) to be held in a timely manner within a period not to exceed 18 months after the transition government assumes power

   (b) with the participation of multiple independent political parties, that have access to the media on an equal basis

   (c) to be conducted under the supervision of internationally recognized observers, such as the Organization of American States, United Nations and other election monitors

(5) has ceased any interference with Radio Martí or Television Martí broadcasts;

(6) makes public commitment to and is making demonstrable progress in

   (a) establishing an independent judiciary

   (b) respecting internationally recognized human rights and basic freedoms as set forth in the Universal Declaration of Human Rights, to which Cuba is a signatory nation

   (c) allowing the establishment of independent trade

unions as set forth in convention 87 and 98 of the International Labor Organization, and allowing the establishment of independent social, economic, and political associations

(7) *does not include Fidel Castro or Raul Castro;**

(8) has given adequate assurance that it will allow the speedy and efficient distribution of assistance to the Cuban people;

(A) *Additional Factors.* In addition to the requirements in sub-section (a) in determining whether a transition government in Cuba is in power, the President shall take into account the extent to which that government

(1) is demonstrably in transition from a communist totalitarian dictatorship to representative democracy;

(2) has made commitments to and is making demonstrable progress in

(a) effectively guaranteeing the rights of free speech and freedom of the press

(b) permitting the reinstatement of citizenship to Cuban-born persons returning to Cuba

(c) assuring the right to of the press private property

(d) *taking the appropriate steps to return to United States citizens (and entities which are fifty percent or more beneficially owned by United States citizens) property taken by the Cuban Government from such citizens and entities on or after January 1, 1959, or to provide equitable compensation to such citizens and entities for such property;**

(3) has extradited or otherwise rendered to the United States all persons sought by the Unites States Department of Justice for crimes committed in the United States and;

(4) has permitted the deployment throughout Cuba of independent and unfettered international human rights monitors.

*Emphasis by author.

Title III is the aspect of the law that has generated the greatest conflict with other nations on the issue of extra-territoriality. It contains a

provision that enables U.S. citizens, former owners of property expropriated by the Cuban government, to sue the current investor in the
property. Any party who "traffics" in those properties could have any
U.S. asset seized to satisfy the findings of the U.S. court. "Trafficking"
is broadly defined and includes selling, leasing, managing, and purchasing expropriated property.

Title IV excludes from the United States—through the denial of
visas—officers of foreign companies that are found to be in violation of
the Helms-Burton Law.

In both laws, the participation of members of the Cuban American
community is well known. The Cuban American National Foundation
(CANF), founded in 1981 under the vigorous and charismatic leadership of Jorge Mas Canosa, decisively built its lobbying capabilities to
back the Torricelli Act and tighten the embargo. On the other hand, the
Helms-Burton Law was formulated by Helms and Burton staffers in
close contact with three Cuban-American members of Congress: Ileana
Ros-Lehtinen and Lincoln Diaz-Baralt of Florida and Robert Menéndez
of New Jersey. The Institute of Democracy in Cuba, the National Association of Sugar Mill Owners of Cuba, and the Bacardi rum company,
who were major property owners prior to the nationalization process
of the 1960s, also participated actively in the drafting of the Helms-
Burton Law.

In January 1998, the publication *Cuba News* from the Miami Herald Publishing Company reported that "to comply with a Helms-Burton
provision that requires the Clinton administration to fund individuals
and non-governmental organizations that support 'democracy-building
efforts in Cuba,' the State Department has disbursed more than US$1.2
million in grants and plans to award more money soon."[3] The funding
is highly concentrated in one county in Florida. This enhances its repre-
sentation in Congress where the rules are based on a first-past-the-post
system. Moreover, the fact that presidents are chosen by the system of
electoral colleges means that each state represents a certain number of
points, based on its population, regardless of the margin with which
they are won. Hence, the Cuban community has been able to deliver a
swing vote in a populous state, thereby enhancing its clout.

The Paradox of Helms-Burton

The Helms-Burton Law in Cuba has had paradoxical results. A law
designed to destroy Fidel Castro has in fact done wonders to rally support for his regime at home and abroad. Cubans may disagree with
their government, and they have been doing so with passion. But the

Cubans will accept any hardship but won't accept masters, as the sign clearly says: "Here, we don't want masters."

Helms-Burton Law has turned much of this disagreement into support. To paraphrase Winston Churchill, the law has convinced them that socialism is the worst of all systems, except for the alternatives. Read from Havana, the U.S. policy has been more concerned with the divisive issue of the property rights of exiles and U.S. corporations than with democracy. While the stated goal is "to assist the Cuban people in regaining their freedom and prosperity," many of its provisions are devoted to property claims.

Cubans are most worried about the provision of the law that allows U.S. citizens (including Cuban-Americans) to file suit in U.S. courts for the equivalent of the value of their confiscated properties since January 1, 1959, plus the accumulated interest to date. This represents several times the current value of those assets. "We can't pay the estimated US$100 billion we supposedly owe to those who left. It represents for us fifty years of exports," says Ricardo Alarcón, president of the National Assembly.

The government has translated the law and made it widely available. It is read and discussed in schools, universities, local organizations, factories, farms, everywhere. It is the source of a new creed and it has rekindled ideology, even among the youngest generation of Cubans born after the revolution who had refused to share the hates and hopes of their parents. Hundreds of students from the University of Havana analyzed 25,000 files from the National Archives, containing the legal proceedings against those accused of embezzlement during the Batista regime before Castro. "By setting this specific date in the Helms-Burton Law, they not only included assets expropriated as a result of the revolution since the Nationalization Law was passed in 1960, but also the assets owned by criminals who fled the country in December 1958," said a twenty-year-old law student to whom, until now, the Batista regime had been only a chapter in history books. Helms-Burton has reunited Cuban society behind the Castro government, deepened the feelings of distrust against the United States, and revived a hundred years of frustrated nationalism.

"If Title III is unacceptable, Title II is an insult," says Ricardo Alarcón, president of the National Assembly. "These Americans, they do not learn. They are now going to tell us how according to *them* we should make a transition and *what* is accepted as a transitional government for them. First, we are not in transition to anything; second, who are they to tell us what we have to do and; third, how can they write in a Law that a transition government should not, I repeat should not include Fidel or Raul Castro? What kind of conditioning over a sovereign country is this?"[4]

Weapon of Choice: The Internal Embargo

If the external embargo has hampered Cuba's growth potential and deepened the feelings of distrust against the United States, the internal embargo has constrained the development of civil, political, and economic freedom for the average Cuban. Freedom is always restricted in periods of war. Usually, countries in a state of war turn inward and become less tolerant of dissent. Wars are not the best times to test new social and political experiments, except for those required by the hostilities.

Much of the intolerance of the Cuban government with the dissident movement is publicly justified with wartime arguments. The Cuban government sees potential Trojan horses behind many demands for liberalization. Private ownership, freedom of the press, and the multiparty system are seen as increasing the political chances of the wealthy enemies in Florida who could regain economic power, fill the country with newspapers and radio stations, and buy electoral support. Losing an election in Cuba would not mean just spending some time in the political opposition in expectation of success the next time around. It would be a total change in the economic, social, and political power structure of society, a major disaster for those now in power. According to the *New York Times*,[5] after a series of hotel bombings in 1997

You can buy a pair of shoes or a picture of Che Guevara in one of Havana's new artisan markets.

organized by radical members of the exile community, a popular saying in Cuba was that just because you're paranoid doesn't mean they aren't out to get you.

The self-employed were perceived as a similar danger. If this group were allowed to expand by renting or purchasing other assets and by hiring workers, then those with rich relatives abroad could act as Trojan horses for the "enemies of the Revolution" and eventually acquire too much power and influence.

The internal embargo imposed by the government has been tragically denying Cubans the access to the freedom and liberty they have long hoped for. The internal embargo is perceived by many as the consequence of Fidel's evil nature. They erroneously believe that it would all end the day after Fidel is out of the picture. But the ending of the internal embargo goes beyond the death or disappearance of Fidel. Just as it would be hard to make sense of a boxer's actions without recognizing that he is anticipating his opponent's moves, it is impossible to understand the internal embargo unless viewed in the context of the long-distance civil war.

The Costs of the War

It's little wonder that income levels collapse in countries at war, including Cuba in its long-distance civil war. On the eve of the revolution,

Cuba ranked near the top in Latin America in many social and economic indicators and enjoyed one of the highest standards of living in the region. In 1957, Cuba ranked second in per capita income behind oil-booming Venezuela. By 1953, seventy-six percent of the population was literate, placing Cuba fourth in literacy after Argentina, Chile, and Costa Rica. Cuba ranked third in average food intake behind Argentina and Uruguay. Only Mexico and Brazil exceeded Cuba in the number of radios owned by individuals (one every 6.5 inhabitants). Cuba was first in per capita telephone consumption (one per thirty-eight), newspaper circulation (one copy per eight inhabitants), private automobile ownership (one to forty) and rail mileage per square mile (one to four).[6] It now lags behind most of the region in all these areas. What happened?

No Trade, No Gain

Is Cuba really hurting from the embargo? While the media often focuses attention on Cuba's inability to import essentials such as medicines and food, this is not the real issue. Since the days of Adam Smith, economists have argued that free trade is good for growth. Recent research has provided ample evidence of this and has even estimated the size of the potential impact. For example, Sachs and Warner[7] show that countries with liberal trading arrangements have grown much faster than those with restricted trade. The Inter-American Development Bank estimated that the trade liberalization carried out in Latin America during the last decade accelerated the region's rate of growth more than one percent per year. This liberalization has involved a reduction in average tariffs from around fifty percent to about fourteen percent. Throughout this process Latin America has had relatively secure access to the U.S. market with very low average tariffs on its exports.

Compared to the distortions created by the embargo, changes in Latin America seem very minor. Hence, if such changes have represented one percent per year in growth for the region, what might the effects on the Cuban economy be of prohibiting access to its natural market for almost forty years? Certainly, several times larger.

Countries in the Caribbean and Central America send over sixty percent of their exports to the United States; Mexico sends over eighty percent. The single most significant negative consequence of the U.S. trade embargo on Cuba has been the limitations it has imposed on Cuba's exports. Cubans could be exporting more citrus, more nickel, more sugar, and more tourism. They would have developed whole new sectors of the economy and capitalized on its educated labor force and its proximity to Florida.

Cuba's tourism has been growing at an astounding rate from US$243 million and 200,000 tourists in 1990 to a gross income of US$1.8 billion and 1.7 million tourists projected for 1998. This is an indication of the sector's potential, and it is happening in spite of the embargo. The United States accounts for the largest share of visitors to the Caribbean. In 1996, 7.2 million U.S. citizens visited the region, 48.5 percent of the total movement of tourists.[8] Imagine Cuba's potential if it could tap into this flow. How much investment and employment would it generate? Total tourism revenues for the Caribbean are estimated at US$14 billion annually. The possibility of lifting the Cuban embargo makes Caribbean tourism agencies nervous. "Cuba is an 800-pound gorilla" said a senior official at one development agency. "Were it to become an attractive destination it could quickly draw as many tourists as all of the smaller islands combined."[9]

Soviet-style communism has demonstrated beyond a reasonable doubt that it is inefficient and Cuba has paid a huge price for adopting such a growth strategy. Nevertheless, the embargo in 1960 forced Cuba to radically shift its export markets and resource allocations in order to integrate itself with a whole set of unnatural trading partners. Then, thirty years later it had to shift again when these countries collapsed. The reallocation of resources to accommodate these changes implied huge economic losses. The weapon of the embargo may not have brought down the government of Cuba, just as it failed to topple either Raul Cédras in Haiti or Saddam Hussein in Iraq. But no one should doubt the magnitude of the economic pain it inflicted or the role it played in Cuba's precipitous fall from its pre-revolutionary development levels.

The Internal Embargo: No Trade in Property or Ideas

Cuban authorities' efforts to ensure that their external enemies would never return to reclaim either their properties or their political influence also had a devastating effect on development prospects. Besides the restrictions on freedom of expression, limitations on the circulation of ideas and on forms of property have prevented Cuba from better mobilizing and using its resources.

Due to the internal embargo, new ideas are considered suspicious. It has become increasingly difficult for academics in general and for economists in particular to freely participate in offering alternatives for future policies. There is an internal embargo on the discussion of issues as important as monetary policy, exchange rate policy, private property, legalization of the small—and medium-sized enterprise, among others.

The self-employed, considered illegal until 1993, have no access to physical space beyond their own homes, or to credit. Nor can they hire workers—only family members can work in the same business. The restrictions on the structure of property rights have hampered the effi-cient allocation of resources. Without the internal embargo, Cubans would be able to buy and sell property, to hire workers, to rent, and to find credit. Resources could flow from less efficient activities to more efficient ones. In short, the Cuban economy would become more effi-cient and productive.

Nationalism and Property Rights: Whose Home Is This Anyway?

Ana Julia had been in Havana for only twenty-four hours and she already knew that things had dramatically changed for the worse. It was June, 1996, the Helms-Burton Law had just been passed in March, and Cubans were outraged with the United States. Academics with ties to U.S. universities were afraid to talk and everyone in Cuba had read the Spanish version of the Law, referred to by the government as "the Law of Slavery" and by many "the Platt Amendment revisited."

Ana Julia had had two unsuccessful meetings with economist friends at the University of Havana: "I'm sorry Anita, but you have to under-stand." Darío, a university professor, was uncomfortably looking around with a mix of fear of being heard and with the helpless shame of an academic who cannot speak freely. "We are suddenly at war, an eco-nomic war has come upon us. All statistics about the Cuban economy are regarded as top secret."

"Darío, the only thing I understand is that you can't tell me what you know. Better times will come when disclosing foreign investment figures will not be a national crime in this country. Let's have a beer and talk about *Guantanamera*.[10] Have you seen the movie?" said Ana Julia changing the subject.

"Of course, who in Cuba hasn't."

The next morning—as had become her routine in past visits to the Island—Ana Julia went to sit in front of what used to be her grandfather's hotel: the San Luis. She loved to sit across the street and look up at the building's run-down, but still beautiful, colonial walls and doors delin-eating the familiar façade. There, in her grandfather's hotel, she had spent the first two years of her life. Again, tears filled her eyes. She could imagine her grandfather walking in his always-white linen suit to get his coffee at the corner. And she could see how the remains of what was once a small *cafeteria* were fighting with collapse. She imagined the night that Batista's secret service came to imprison her father while she was in his arms on the same balcony she could see from across the street. How different life would have been for all of us if the revolution had never happened? Who knows! she thought, shrugging her shoulders. She realized that she did not care to imagine that. Ana Julia did not want revenge, like many other Cubans, nor did she hate anyone. She remembered Virginia's words, "In spite of all the mistakes, all the frustration, the sufferings and the setbacks, I am convinced today, that the revolution just had to happen." Maybe she was right. But now Cuba needed to leave the revolution behind and look to the future, come to terms with the past as she had done.

"Did you come to get the information you need to sue us in the United States and get your hotel back?" a strong voice from across the street interrupted her thoughts. It was a group of people Ana knew from other trips. They lived in the building and had been living there for twenty years. She had met them before. She had sipped coffee with them many times, remembering the days her family lived within the same walls they now called their homes.

"What's the matter with you guys?" she dared to ask them. "Hey! It's me, remember?"

"We know it's you. You're Cruz's granddaughter, and with the Helms-Burton Law you can get your hotel back," a young man told Ana defiantly.

She crossed the street towards the group of people standing like guards in front of the deteriorated façade. "Listen, first of all I am not a U.S. citizen. Second, it doesn't apply in your case and third, even if it did, I wouldn't do it. I'm against the Helms-Burton Law. I don't think it solves anything. It just deepens what keeps us apart and I want to get closer, not further." Ana put an arm around one of them and said, "Would you do something like that?"

"Never, this is our home."

Ana remembered her grandfather's words to the *miliciano* back in 1960 before he left Cuba for good. They had been exactly the same: "This hotel is my home. I have lived here with my family for fifteen years."

No, not again, she thought. Let's end this fight. "*Viejo*," she joked to the building administrator, "One day, when the government lets us, I'm going to make you an offer you can't refuse and I'm going to buy this old place from you and turn it into a hotel again."

"Well, if the price is right, we might accept the offer," they answered.

TABLE 9.1   Cuba and the Socialist Bloc: % GDP Plunge and Recovery

	1990	1991	1992	1993	1994	1995	1996	1997
Russia	−3.4	−13.1	−14.5	−8.7	−12.6	−4.0	−6.0	n.a.
Ukraine	−3.3	−11.3	−13.7	−14.2	−19.0	−4.0	−10.0	n.a.
Poland	−11.6	−7.6	1.5	3.8	5.2	7.1	6.0	5.0
Hungary	−3.3	−7.4	−3.0	−0.6	2.9	1.5	0.2	2.0
Rumania	−6.5	−13.2	−8.8	1.5	3.9	6.9	3.5	0.1
Cuba	−2.9	−10.7	−11.6	−14.9	0.7	2.5	7.8	3.0

Sources: International Bank for Reconstruction and Development, World Tables, Baltimore: Johns Hopkins University Press, 1955; IMF: Poland: The Path to a Market Economy, Washington, D.C., October 1994; Banco Nacional de Cuba; Monthly Bulletin of Statistics, United Nations, New York, 1998.

When Will It End?

In general, civil wars end in one of two ways. Either you win, or you negotiate. The current U.S. policy is based on a scenario of total victory, a la the Berlin Wall. This scenario is vividly described in the Helms-Burton Act. The embargo will be maintained and strengthened until Cubans overthrow Fidel Castro and his brother Raul, call elections within eighteen months, and commit to return the properties that were expropriated since 1959 (Title II, Section 205). The Cuban lobby has been particularly vigilant in preventing any relaxation of U.S. restrictions and even protested the re-establishment of direct flights and of the right to send remittances in March, 1998.

This scenario of total victory looked plausible in 1993 when an economic collapse seemed inevitable, prompting Andrés Oppenheimer to name his book *Fidel's Final Hour.* However, the Cuban economic reforms adopted since then seem to assure a path of moderate growth, even if the long-distance civil war continues.

True, the collapse in economic activity after the fall of the Soviet Union was enormous. However, it was of the same order of magnitude as the one experienced in Eastern Europe. And its recuperation has been much more rapid.

No Longer on the Brink of Collapse

Cuba is no longer on the brink of collapse:

- The economic reforms implemented since 1990 have promoted growth in non-traditional sectors like tourism, which has become the main source of hard currency. In 1989, sugar represented seventy-two percent of dollar exports while tourism accounted for only four percent. By 1997, the situation had changed dramatically with tourism accounting for forty-four percent (US$1.5 billion) of gross dollar income while sugar had been relegated to second place with twenty-six percent, or US$900 million, in exports.

- The flow of remittances has been growing constantly and is expected to reach US$1 billion in 1998.

- Foreign investment has been growing, mainly in the form of joint ventures with the Cuban government. An estimated US$2.1 billion in foreign investment from over twenty-five different countries had been announced by 1997.

- Cuba is thriving on state capitalism. Decentralization of big government enterprises and foreign investment are helping change the mentality of managers, workers, and politicians.

- Private capitalism, however, is a different story. Those self-employed that work in authorized services are better described as land rafters than emerging capitalists. Struggling to grow without capital and resources, the self-employed have been legalized but not legitimized.

Thus, Cuba does not seem to be facing a meltdown but rather a period of moderate recovery. Apparently, the attempt to tighten the noose around the Cuban economy's neck has not succeeded. But if the embargo were to succeed in generating economic ruin, the United States risks massive and uncontrolled emigration from Cuba. This scenario would face too much opposition in the United States and make Cuba policy a concern for the general public rather than just the Cuban lobby. For this reason, a total victory for the exiles is unlikely.

By the same token, a total victory for Fidel is not in the cards. The Cuban lobby would have to lose all its influence on U.S. policy and receive nothing in exchange. The exile community has already lost everything it had in Cuba; it has too little else to lose to just lay down its guns.

A negotiated settlement, similar to those that ended the civil wars

in Nicaragua, El Salvador, and Guatemala, might have increasing support. In those cases, there were in principle no winners or losers. The
left-wing guerrillas of El Salvador and Guatemala won major reforms
of the political system in the areas of human rights, political participation, amnesty, and social programs in exchange for laying down their
arms. The opposition forces of Nicaragua got a chance at an open election process, an opportunity that delivered them a victory.

Support for a negotiated settlement may come from many quarters.
First, other American interests, including the business sector, may ad-
vocate a different policy towards Cuba, wresting parliamentary control
from the Cuban lobby. Second, demographic changes within the Cuban
exile community may give less weight to the interests of the few wealthy
individuals that might benefit from the property provisions of the Helms-
Burton Act and more towards more recent immigrants with closer ties
to families in Cuba. Finally, the increasing number of Cubans engaged
in market-oriented activities might press for a chance at opportunities
foregone by the embargo.

The long-distance civil war is not over. But the sharp demarcation
between those who left and those who stayed has blurred. In Cuba, a
taste of capitalism and freedom has whet the appetite of many and created a constituency for further liberalization. Among exiles, the hunger
for revenge has waned with the pain of years of separation from family,
friends, and home. More and more people on both sides are searching
for a way—a way to end the battle, a way for Cuba to grow, a way to
have both freedom and equity—a Cuban way.

Notes

1. Karl Von Clausewitz, *War, Politics, & Power* (Chicago: Regnery, 1962),
   1. Translated by Edward M. Collins.
2. Sir Winston Churchill, Speech at the House of Commons, July 2, 1942.
   In *The International Thesaurus of Quotations* (New York: HarperCollins
   Publishers, Inc., 1996).
3. Among the beneficiaries of the grants are: "Freedom House, a New York-
   based human rights group that until recently was headed by Cuban exile
   Frank Calzón, US$500,000; the Institute for Democracy in Cuba, a coa-
   lition of ten anti-Castro groups whose leaders include Nick Gutiérrez, a
   Miami attorney who says he helped write the Helms-Burton property
   sanctions, is slated to receive US$400,000; the U.S.-Cuba Business Coun-
   cil, a group headed by former Ambassador Otto Reich, a Cuban exile
   who works on property claims against Cuba; the Cuban Revolutionary
   Democratic Directorate, headed by Cuban American engineer Juan José
   Fernández de Castro, who seeks support for its anti-Castro movement

in Latin America." The same note states "the Helms-Burton grants were championed by Rep. Robert Menéndez, a Cuban-American Democrat who represents the New Jersey district." *See Cuba News* 6, no. 1 (January 1998): 5.

4. Conversation with Ricardo Alarcón, June 1996. *See* Title II of the Helms-Burton Law for these specific provisions called "requirements and factors for determining a transition government."

5. *See* "Key Cuban Foe Claims Exiles' Baking," in *The New York Times,* July 12, 1998.

6. *See* Louis Pérez, *Cuba: Between Reform and Revolution.*

7. Integration and Trade in the Americas: Inter-American Development Bank, Department of Integration and Regional Programs, Periodic Note, Washington, D.C., August 1998.

8. Caribbean Report, *Miami Herald,* January 15, 1998.

9. For more information, *see* Erik D'Amato, "Travel's Economic Impact," *Latin Finance* (June 1997).

10. A humorous Cuban film highly critical of the socialist bureaucracy and the government. Directed by Tomas Gutierrez Alea and Juan Carlos Tavio. Released in 1996.

BIBLIOGRAPHY

Asamblea Nacional del Poder Popular. *Debates y Decisiones del Parlamento Cubano*, Havana, May 1994.

Agence France Presse, February 1998.

Banco Nacional de Cuba, Economic Report, 1994.

Quote from Juan Jose Gaitero, director-general of Voltor Engineering and Equipment SA, in a *Bohemia* interview, August 14, 1995.

Burns, E. Bradford. *Latin America: A Concise Interpretive History.* Englewood Cliffs: Prentice Hall, 1994.

Cardoso, Eliana and Helwege, Ann. *Cuba after Communism.* Cambridge, Mass.: MIT Press, 1992.

Carranza, Julio. "Cuba: Los Retos de la Economia." *Cuadernos de Nuestra America,* no. 19, 1992.

Carranza, Gutierrez y Monreal. *Cuba: la Reestructuración de la Economía,* Editorial de Ciencias Sociales, La Habana, 1995.

Carranza, Gutierrez and Monreal. *Cuba: Restructuring the Economy: A Contribution to the Debate.* London: The Institute of Latin American Studies, University of London, 1996.

Carrol, Lewis. *Alice in Wonderland.* New York: Scholastic Paperbacks, 1988.

Castañeda, Jorge. *La Vida en Rojo.* Alfaguara, Mexico, 1997.

Castro, Fidel. Speech at the National Assembly. December 28, 1993.

Centro de Estudios de la Economia Cubana (CEEC). *La Economia en 1996: Resultados y Perspectivas Havana.* University of Havana, 1997.

CEPAL Report. *Cuba: Evolucion Economica Durante 1994.*

CEPAL. *La Economia Cubana: reformas estructurales y desempeno en los noventa.* Mexico: Fondo de Cultura Economica, 1997.

Cockcroft, James D. *Neighbors in Turmoil: Latin America.* New York: Harper & Row, Publishers, 1989.

Cohn, Evelyn and Berlin, Alan. "European Community Reacts to Helms-Burton." *New York Law Journal* (August 4, 1997): S2.

Collins, Paul. "Cuba: Crisis and the Road to Recovery" in Heath, John, ed. *Revitalizing Socialist Enterprise: A Race Against Time.* London: Routledge Publishing, 1993.

Columbia Journal of World Business, March 22, 1995.

Cuban Foreign Investment Act.

CUBAInfo 9, no. 10 (July 31, 1997).

CUBAInfo 8, no. 4 (March 21, 1996).

Deutsche Presse-Agentur, July 11, 1996.

D'Amato, Erik. "Travel's Economic Impact." *Latin Finance,* June 1997.

DeGeorge, Gail. "A Touch of Capitalism." *Business Week,* no. 3518 (March

17, 1997).

Detroit Business, June 6, 1994.

Dominguez, Jorge I. "The Political Impact of Cuba on the Reform and Collapse of Communist Regimes." In Mesa-Lago, Carmelo, ed. *Cuba after the Cold War.* Pittsburgh: University of Pittsburgh Press, 1993.

———. "Cuban Politics Before and After the 1991 Communist Party Congress." In Pérez-Lopez, Jorge, ed. *Cuba at a Crossroads: Politics and Economics after the Fourth Party Congress.* Gainesville: University Press of Florida, 1994.

The Economist. Cuba Survey. April 1996.

Export Control News 8, no. 9 (September 30, 1994).

Financial Times, February 17, 1989.

———, June 11, 1992.

———, October 27, 1995.

———, June 20, 1997.

Gazeta Oficial de la Republica de Cuba, Numero 5, Extraordinaria. September 8, 1993. Radio Progreso, Havana, 1143 gmt, September 9, 1993.

Gerchunoff, Pablo. "Peronist Economic Policies, 1946–55." In de Tella, Guido and Dornbusch, Rudiger, eds. *The Political Economy of Argentina, 1946–83.* Pittsburgh: University of Pittsburgh Press, 1989.

González Nuñez, Gerardo. "La Economia Cubana entre la Urgencia y la Meditación: Algunas Reflexiones sobre la Despenalización de la Divisa." Centros de Estudios Sobre America (CEA), Havana, 1994.

Granma, July 1986.

———, National Assembly Debates, December 28, 1993.

Halebsky, Sandor and Harris, Richard, eds. *Capital, Power, and Inequality in Latin America.* Boulder, CO: 1995.

Hays, Dennis. "Cuba's HIV Quarantine Takes Toll in Liberty; Medicine from US." *New York Times* (July 30, 1993): A26.

Heath, John, ed. *Revitalizing Socialist Enterprise: A Race Against Time.* London: Routledge Publishing, 1993.

Hilliker, Grant. *The Politics of Reform in Peru.* Baltimore: The Johns Hopkins University Press, 1971.

Hodges, Donald C. *Argentina, 1943–1987: The National Revolution and Resistance.* Albuquerque: University of New Mexico Press, 1988.

Horowitz, Irving Louis, ed. *Cuban Communism, 7th edition.* New Brunswick: Transaction Publishers, 1989.

Informe Económico, Ministerio de Economía y Planificación de Cuba, Primer Semestre 1996.

Ing, David. "Spanish Chain Nixes Cuba Deal." *Hotel and Motel Management,* July 22, 1996.

Instituto Americano Para el Desarollo del Sindicalismo Libre, AFL-CIO. "Inversionistas Extranjeras: lubricando la maquinaria gubernamental Cubana." Washington, DC, February 13, 1995.

Jimenez, Alexis Codina. "Worker Incentives in Cuba." In Zimbalist, Andrew, ed. *Cuba's Socialist Economy Toward the 1990s.* Boulder, CO: Lynne Rienner, 1987.

Kenen, Joanne. "US Medical Team Finds Embargo Hurts Cuban Health." *The Reuter European Business Report.* March 3, 1997.

Kirkpatrick, A.F. "For Over Thirty Years the Embargo by the USA has Restricted Cuba's Ability to Purchase Food and Medicines." *The Lancet,* November 30, 1996.

The Lancet 39, no. 48 (February 1, 1997).

Latin American Newsletters, September 1, 1994.

Latin American Telecom Report, July 1, 1994.

Law and Policy in International Business, September 21, 1995.

LDC Debt Report/Latin American Markets, November 15, 1993.

———, April 18, 1994.

Malloy, James, ed. *Beyond the Revolution: Bolivia Since 1952.* Pittsburgh: University of Pittsburgh Press, 1971.

Marquis, Christopher. "Cuban Economy Feels Blow of US Law." *The New York Times* (November 28, 1996): A1.

Mesa-Lago, Carmelo. *The Economy of Socialist Cuba: A Two-Decade Appraisal.* Albuquerque: University of New Mexico Press, 1981.

———, ed. *Cuba after the Cold War.* Pittsburgh: University of Pittsburgh Press, 1993.

Miami Herald interview with Jose Manuel Vivanco, director of the Americas Division of Human Rights Watch, January 26, 1989.

Miami Herald, Caribbean Report, January 15, 1997.

Monmany, Terence. "Study Criticizes Virtual Medical Embargo on Cuba." *Los Angeles Times,* July 24, 1997.

Morley, Morris. *Imperial State and Revolution: the United States and Cuba, 1952–1986.* Cambridge: Cambridge University Press, 1987.

Murdock, Deroy. "Cuba: This Island of Lost Potential." *World Trade* 10, no. 8 (August 1997): 28-31.

Nieves, Silvia Domenech. "Cuba's Economy During the Special Period in Peacetime: Changes and Transformations." Havana: Prensa Latina News Agency, March 29, 1995.

New York Times, January 12, 1993.

Oppenheimer, Andrés. *Castro's Final Hour: The Secret Behind the Coming Downfall of Communist Cuba.* New York: Simon & Schuster, 1992.

Paterson, Thomas. *Contesting Castro: The United States and the Triumph of the Cuban Revolution.* New York: Oxford University Press, 1994.

Pérez, Louis. *Cuba: Between Reform and Revolution.* New York: Oxford University Press, 1955.

Perez, Omar. "El Comercio Exterior y la Inversión Extranjera en la Economía Cubana." In *La Economía Cubana en 1996.* CEEC, University of Havana, 1997.

Pérez-Lopez, Jorge. *Cuba's Second Economy.* New Brunswick: Transaction Publishers, 1995.

Platt's Oilgram News, February 12, 1993.

Prensa Latina interview with Cuban Foreign Investment and Economic Cooperation minister Ernesto Melendez, June 10, 1995.

The Reuter Business Report, July 4, 1996.

Reuters, June 6, 1986.

———, February 22, 1993.

———, September 28, 1993.

———, Caribbean Update, November 1994.

Reuters World Service, April 24, 1996.

Riggs, Susan. "Will Obscure Canadian Law Bring the US Policy to Heel?" *The*

Baltimore Sun (January 5, 1997): 5F.

Rock, David. *Argentina, 1516–1982: From Spanish Colonization to the Falklands War.* Berkeley: University of California Press, 1985.

Rodríguez, Carlos. "El Nuevo Camino de la Agricultura Cubana." *Cuba Socialista,* no. 27, Havana, 1963.

Rodríguez, José Luis. *Estrategia del Desarrollo Economico en Cuba.* Havana: Editorial de Ciencias Sociales, 1990.

———. Speech at World Economic Forum. In Davos, Switzerland, February 1996.

———. *La Economia Cubana: Situación en 1997 y Perspectivas.* ECLAC Conference, Mexico City, October 1997.

Sanz, Marie. "US Increasingly Isolated over Cuba Policy." Agence France Presse, November 13, 1996.

Schlesinger, Stephen and Kinzer, Stephen. *Bitter Fruit: The Untold Story of the American Coup in Guatemala.* Garden City, New York: Anchor Books, 1983.

Szulc, Tad. *Fidel: A Critical Portrait.* New York: William Morrow and Company, 1986.

Skidmore, Thomas and Smith, Peter. *Modern Latin America.* New York: Oxford University Press, 1997.

Terrero, Ariel. "Tendencias de un Ajuste." *Bohemia,* October 26, 1994.

Theriot, Lawrence. "Cuba Faces the Economic Realities of the 1980s." In Horowitz, Irving Louis, ed. *Cuban Communism, 7th edition.* New Brunswick: Transaction Publishers, 1989.

U.S. Department of the Treasury. Office of Foreign Assets Control. "An Analysis of Licensed Trade With Cuba By Foreign Subsidiaries of U.S. Companies." July 1993.

Vargas, Jorge. Cuba: Foreign Investment Act of 1995. Introductory Note in the *Loyola of Los Angeles International and Comparative Law Journal,* 1996.

The Washington Post, October 5, 1981.

The Washington Post, May 23, 1995.

Walte, J. "US Urged to Ease Cuban Embargo." *USA Today,* March 7, 1995.

Wenge, Ralph. "Helms-Burton Act Puts Pressure on Companies in Cuba." CNN World Report, November 13, 1996.

Wiarda, Howard and Kline, Harvey, eds. *Latin American Politics and Development.* Boulder, CO: Westview Press, 1985.

Zimbalist, Andrew, ed. *Cuba's Socialist Economy Toward the 1990s.* Boulder, CO: Lynne Reinner Publishers, 1987.

———. "Reforming Cuba's Economic System from Within." In Pérez-Lopez, Jorge, ed. *Cuba at a Crossroads: Politics and Economics after the Fourth Party Congress.* Gainesville: University Press of Florida, 1994.

——— and Eckstein, Susan. "Patterns of Cuban Development: The First Twenty-five Years." In Zimbalist, Andrew, ed. *Cuba's Socialist Economy Toward the 1990s.*

INDEX

Page references followed by t, f, or n indicate tables, figures, or endnotes.
References in *italics* indicate photographs.

JOANNA HAUSMANN JATAR

ABOUT THE AUTHOR

Ana Julia Jatar-Hausmann is a Senior Fellow at the Inter-American
Dialogue in Washington, D.C., where she has been doing research on
Cuba and traveled often to the island, at times as part of the institute's
Cuba Task Force. She is an economist with a Ph.D. from the University
of Warwick, U.K. Dr. Jatar is a Venezuelan citizen born in Cuba. She
fled the island in 1953 with her family, not to return until 1995, when
she was inspired to begin work on this book. She was a Lecturer at
Venezuela's leading Graduate School of Business (1986–92) and also
served as Venezuela's first Director of Pro-Competencia (the anti-trust
agency) from 1992 to 1994 and as General Director for Planning and
Coordinator of the VII National Plan in the Planning Ministry (1984–
85). Dr. Jatar has been invited to lecture on Cuba at the School of
International Affairs at Harvard University, the North-South Center
at the University of Miami and at Georgetown University in
Washington, D.C. Dr. Jatar has been a frequent source on Cuba for
The Economist, BBC World Service, Radio Martí, Union Radio and
has debated with leading Cuban exile figures on the U.S. Spanish TV
channel Univision and CNBC. She has also testified before the U.S.
House of Representatives on the state of Cuban economic reforms.

Books of related interest
from Kumarian Press

Promises Not Kept:
The Betrayal of Social Change in the Third World

Fourth Edition
John Isbister

This book develops the argument that social change in the Third World has been blocked by a series of broken promises, made explicitly or implicitly by the industrialized countries and also by Third World leaders themselves.

The fourth edition takes into account the success stories in the Third World, particularly in East Asia, asking why those experiences have not been more widespread.

US$21.95 / Paper: 1-56549-078-9

The Human Farm:
A Tale of Changing Lives and Changing Lands

Katie Smith

A detailed account of how people, under the leadership of Jose Elias Sanchez, have achieved more than agricultural development, learning basic skills and receiving encouragement that renews the spirit, provides hope, and leads to a new sense of community—a human transformation

US$14.95 / Paper: 0-56549-039-8
US$30.00 / Cloth: 0-56549-040-1

Mediating Sustainability:
Growing Policy from the Grassroots

Editors: Jutta Blauert and Simon Zadek

This book explores how mediation between grass-roots and policy formation processes works in practice by focusing on experiences in Latin America in promoting sustainable agriculture and rural development. The contributions to this book draw on the work of researchers, activists, farmers and policy makers through concrete evidence and appraisal.

US$25.95 Paper: 1-56549-081-9
US$55.00 Cloth: 1-56549-082-7

Knowledge Shared:
Participatory Evaluation in Development Cooperation

Edward T. Jackson
Yusuf Kassam

This book examines an approach to evaluation that enables citizens and professionals alike to jointly assess the extent to which the benefits of development are shared—and by whom. It presents leading-edge analysis on the theory and practice of participatory evaluation around the world.

US$25.95 / Paper: 1-56549-085-1

 Kumarian Press is dedicated to publishing and distributing books and other media that will have a positive social and economic impact on the lives of peoples living in "Third World" conditions no matter where they live.

Kumarian Press publishes books about Global Issues and International Development, such as Peace and Conflict Resolution, Environmental Sustainability, Globalization, Nongovernmental Organizations, and Women and Gender.

To receive a complimentary catalog or to request writer's guidelines call or write:

Kumarian Press, Inc.
14 Oakwood Avenue
West Hartford, CT 06119-2127
U.S.A.

Inquiries: (860) 233-5895
Fax: (860) 233-6072
Order toll free: (800) 289-2664

e-mail: kpbooks@aol.com
Internet: www.kpbooks.com